# Clocks and Watches

## HUGH TAIT

Published for the Trustees of the British Museum b...

**BRITISH MUSEUM PUBLICATIONS**

*previous page*
Three watches with
enamelled cases, 1777-1878:
(*from left to right*) the watch
and chatelaine made for Sir
James Napier, F.R.S., F.S.A.,
enamelled by William Craft
in the neo-classical style,
including the heads of King
George III and his consort,
and containing a quarter-
repeating movement by John
Leroux of Charing Cross,
London (length 6¾ in,
17.1 cm), *purchased in 1979*;
a Swiss watch decorated
with pearls and enamelled
floral designs; the movement
(shown out of its case,
*centre*), also enamelled and
elaborately engraved, signed
*Bovet Fleurier*, is the version
of the duplex escapement
that was invented by C.F. Jacot
in 1830 and often used by the
Bovet firm in their exports to
China in the middle of the
nineteenth century, *from the
Ilbert Collection*; an
exceptionally elaborate
striking watch with lever
escapement made in 1878 for
Sir John Bennett, whose firm
had been active in London
from 1843, the case being
enamelled in the neo-Gothic
style with armorial devices,
*purchased 1980*.

*right*
Detail of the dials and hoods
of three early long-case clocks
made in London, *c.* 1665–80;
see *inside back cover*.

© 1983 The Trustees of the British Museum
ISBN 0 7141 2022 7
Published by British Museum Publications,
46 Bloomsbury Street, London WC1B 3QQ
Designed and produced by Roger
Set in Zapf Light
Printed in Italy by New Interlitho

**THE TRUSTEES OF THE BRITISH MUSEUM
acknowledge with gratitude the generosity of
THE HENRY MOORE FOUNDATION
for the grant which made possible
the publication of this book**

# Contents

# Preface

In 1958, the celebrated Ilbert Collection was saved for the nation chiefly through the outstanding generosity of Mr Gilbert Edgar, C.B.E., and the efforts of the Worshipful Company of Clockmakers, and added to the already impressive accumulation of Renaissance clocks, watches and scientific instruments at the British Museum. Overnight, one of the world's finest concentrations of material for the systematic study of horology was created in the very heart of London.

Exactly twenty years ago, a specially equipped Students' Room for Horology and Scientific Instruments, with an adjoining workshop and a skilled craftsman in attendance, was opened at the British Museum to enable the interested enthusiast – apprentices and scholars, collectors and historians, experimenters and amateur makers alike – to tap the seemingly inexhaustible riches of this vast collection of some three thousand items. Since then, the Room itself has been extended and the nucleus of a specialist horological library provided by a generous gift from Courtenay Ilbert's nephew, Mr Michael Inchbald, has been transformed into a fine reference 'tool', rich both in publications and photographic archives. The workshop facilities, so essential for the proper care and cataloguing of the mechanisms, have been steadily improved but, most importantly, a team of four skilled horologists now maintain a regular weekday service in the Students' Room.

Without the continuing work of my colleagues in the horological team, my task in writing this book would have been much more difficult – and my thanks go particularly to Richard Good, the Superintendent of the Students' Room, whose profound knowledge and first-hand expertise of precision clockwork and of modern developments in mechanical watchwork is truly invaluable and whose advice is always so freely given; to Jeremy Evans, Senior Conservation Officer, who generously discussed with me his research on the cockle shell group of 'turret' clocks and other early clocks in the Collections; to David Thompson, Research Assistant, for checking innumerable factual details and organising the smooth-running but lengthy photographic sessions and to Christopher Worsley, Museum Assistant, for his work on the index.

The colour illustrations with the exception of figs. 17a, 40–41 were all specially taken for this book by a member of the Museum's staff, Mr Tony Milton, Senior Photographer, and I would like to record my special thanks for his determined efforts to capture the many diverse, even conflicting aspects of these complex objects. We are indebted to Mr Lee Boltin for fig. 17a and to a former colleague, Mr Beresford Hutchinson, for the execution of the line drawings and the model of the mechanism of the Burgundian late medieval clock (fig. 20).

# Introduction

A clock or a watch? Nowadays, most people make the simple distinction that a watch, unlike a clock, is designed to be carried or worn on the person. In this book, this popular criterion will be followed although until quite recently it would have been considered unacceptable.

In the past a clock was the name reserved for a mechanical timepiece that strikes the hours in passing, for the word derives from the Latin clocca – a bell. A particularly early and most explicit use of the English word clock occurs in a medieval Latin manuscript record of a works account of 1375–7, when a new bell was provided for King Edward III's clock in Windsor Castle; it reads:

'a great bell called Edward bought for a certain horologe called clokke (pro quodam horilagio vocato clokke) within the said castle of Windsor.'

However, there were, as there are today, many timepieces which possessed the general appearance of clocks although they lacked a striking mechanism and, conversely, there were many seemingly straightforward watches which struck the hours in passing and should, in consequence, have been more correctly described as 'clocks' – indeed, the English compromised by naming them 'clock-watches'.

In this short account of the clocks and watches in the British Museum only a very small percentage are described and illustrated. The choice fell on those which best demonstrated the main stages of development in the evolution of the mechanical timepiece since the Middle Ages. There are, however, two ways of looking at clocks and watches, either from the outside or from the inside. Because the clockmaker was always seeking to improve the accuracy of his timepiece, he introduced changes in the construction of the mechanism which necessitated changes in the outward appearance. The extent to which the outward design of the clock and the watch is related to its mechanical construction is discussed within this brief survey, but a recurring pattern emerging over the centuries indicates that, again and again, the clockmaker's concern for greater accuracy in timekeeping has flaunted and triumphed over current tastes of fashion and case design until in 1955 the almost unimaginable accuracy of one second in 300 years was attained by the so-called 'atomic-clock', at the National Physical Laboratory, Teddington, in which no concessions to outward appearances are made.

# 1 Weight-driven 'Frame' Clocks

**5** Richard of Wallingford, Abbot of St Albans (1327–36), depicted standing beside his renowned astronomical clock. In this Latin manuscript list of benefactors of the Abbey, the illuminator, one Alan Strayler, has shown Richard's face in its diseased state. *British Library* (MS Cotton Nero D. VII, fol. 20 recto).

The first mechanical clock to be made does not survive. Indeed, neither the inventor, nor the place nor the date of the first mechanical clock is known, but by about AD 1300 most European countries, England, France, Italy and Germany, had some form of mechanical clock in regular use – that is to say, a weight-driven timepiece with a bell.

Until the Gothic Middle Ages, man had measured time by such devices as 'shadow-clocks' or sun-dials, water-clocks or 'clepsydrae'. The Babylonian and ancient Egyptian civilisations, followed by the Greek and Roman cultures, depended on these non-mechanical means for measuring time. From the beginning of the Christian era until long after the invention of the mechanical clock towards the end of the thirteenth century, the scribes use the same Latin word, *horologium*, to denote any instrument concerned with the recording of time, be it a sundial, a water-clock, or a mechanical weight-driven clock, and consequently the early entries so far traced in the surviving records are frequently ambiguous. In themselves, these entries rarely provide evidence of the exact date of a change over to a weight-driven mechanical clock. However, the absence of any reference to mechanical clocks in two important thirteenth-century works – the *Computus maior* written by Campanus for Pope Urban IV between about 1261 and 1264 and the *Liber del Saber Astronomico* produced for Alfonso X of Castille in 1277 – has led historians to the tentative conclusion that the mechanical clock was probably not invented before about 1280. As the number of significant records which may plausibly be interpreted as referring to mechanical clocks increases rapidly during the next fifty years, it would seem that few of the great monasteries, abbey churches and cathedrals in Europe had not set about installing some kind of mechanical clock with a bell before the middle of the fourteenth century. A document of 1302 from the rich Benedictine Abbey at Ely, for example, makes it clear that the monks were to assemble for prayer at the correct times during the day and night with the assistance of a clock, which had to be kept in good order for that purpose. Between 1321 and 1325, another powerful Benedictine abbey in East Anglia was paying two clockmakers, Roger of Stoke and Laurence, to build a particularly fine clock for the Cathedral in Norwich. It took nearly three years to complete, but it seems to have had additional dials for the sun and the moon and may also have had an alarum mechanism.

With the Gothic invention, the timekeeping was, for the first time, governed by a repetitive mechanical motion lasting as long as a driving force was maintained. This driving force in those earliest days of clockmaking was provided by weights and the brilliance of the new invention lay in the fact that it could control and slow down the speed at which the weights dropped. The mechanism for slowing down and evening out the spending of this power from the weights

**2** The Cassiobury Park Clock: a weight-driven iron 'tower' (or 'turret') clock in the medieval tradition. This view shows the going-train, with the crown-wheel, verge and foliot clearly visible. The striking-train has been removed for the sake of clarity. Height 30 in (76 cm). *Purchased in 1964.*

**3** The Cassiobury Park Clock: a view showing the striking-train, with the count-wheel clearly visible in the centre. The going-train has been removed for the sake of clarity.

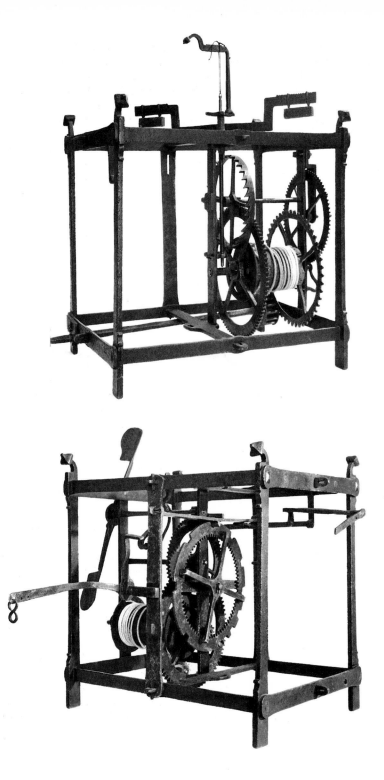

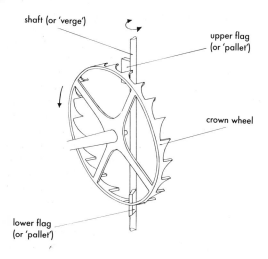

shaft (or 'verge')

upper flag (or 'pallet')

crown wheel

lower flag (or 'pallet')

**1** Diagram illustrating the 'verge' escapement.

was called an 'escapement'. The earliest surviving form of an escapement has come to be known as the 'verge escapement' and it was one of those great and fundamental inventions which have profoundly affected the history of man.

The verge escapement remained the only form of escapement generally used in all clocks and watches until about 1670, nearly four centuries after its successful, but as yet anony-

**4** The Cassiobury Park Clock: a detail showing the punch-mark, a cockleshell, stamped on the central cross-bar of the iron frame. Length ⅝ in (1.6 cm). NB This mark occurs on at least four other 'turret' clocks of similar iron construction, and, as this group seems to have been originally located in the area between St Albans and Cambridge, it may be the mark of a local clockmaker who was working in the medieval tradition, perhaps during the sixteenth century, if not earlier.

mous, application to the problem of time-measurement. The verge escapement consists of three parts, which can be most clearly seen and understood in the large 'turret' clock from Cassiobury Park (*figs. 2 – 4*), which, like the Dover Castle clock (now in the Science Museum, London), was formerly thought to have been made in the fourteenth century. Both are now regarded as probably no older than the sixteenth century. Nevertheless, the method of construction of this clock, with its massive heavy wrought-iron frame and mechanism, is in the medieval tradition and scarcely differs from the oldest surviving clock in Britain – the Salisbury Cathedral clock of 1386.

The three parts of which the verge consists (*fig. 1*) are, firstly, the 'crown-wheel', a wheel with an uneven number of teeth standing at an angle of 90° to the plane of the wheel; secondly, a shaft (or 'verge') on which are two rectangular projections known as 'flags' (or 'pallets'); and thirdly, at the top end of the shaft either a horizontal bar called a 'foliot' (*fig. 2*) or a large wheel called a 'balance' (*figs. 11 – 12*). The action of the escapement is very simple: as the weight is applied to the 'going-train' of wheels meshing one into the other, the crown-wheel is turned. The top pallet is thereby pushed aside by a tooth on the moving crown-wheel and in consequence the verge is turned and so is the foliot on top of the shaft. During this turn the tooth of the crown-wheel 'escapes' from contact with the top pallet; at the same moment, the lower pallet is caught by a tooth on the lower part of the crown-wheel, which is of course moving in the opposite direction to the top of the wheel. Because there are an uneven number of teeth on the crown-wheel, when the lower pallet is engaged by a tooth, the upper pallet will coincide with a space between two teeth. The verge is impelled to move in one direction by the force of the tooth of the crown-wheel on the pallet until it escapes, at which moment the other pallet becomes engaged by a tooth on the opposite side of the crown-wheel, so impelling the verge to revolve in the opposite direction.

The speed of this turning motion backwards and forwards is adjustable, either by applying a different weight to the going-train of the clock, or by moving the tiny weights on the foliot further out on the arm (to make it slower) or closer in on the arm (to make it swing faster). This control of the speed of the movement enables the clock to be adjusted for more accurate time-keeping but the degree of error in these movements was always very considerable – indeed, without a semi-permanent attendant none of these public clocks would have been reliable. Thus, one of the earliest references in England occurs in 1370 with the payment of wages at sixpence a day to one John Nicole, 'keeper of the great clock of the lord king within the palace of Westminster'.

The first mechanical clock about which detailed and precise technical information has survived was made in an English Benedictine monastery and was the creation of Richard of Wallingford, who from 1327 until his death in 1336 was Abbot of St Albans. He has subsequently been recognised as the most famous English mathematician and astronomer of the Middle Ages (*fig. 5*). Although his very large and justly renowned astronomical clock, showing the motions of the sun, moon and planets, lunar eclipses, etc., has not been seen since John Leland described it in Henry VIII's reign, the original Latin texts in manuscript have recently been traced, translated and critically studied by Dr John North – with profound and fundamental results. A model of the escapement of the St Albans Clock, based on the dimensions laid down by Richard of Wallingford, was made by Mr Peter Haward in 1973 (*fig. 6*) and is now exhibited beside the Cassiobury Park Clock because it demonstrates the alternative form of the verge escapement used in England in the early fourteenth century. In place of the ubiquitous version of the verge-and-foliot escapement associated with all medieval 'turret' clocks, which has just been described, the St Albans Clock had, in addition to a verge with a foliot carrying weights, *two* escape-wheels – not one crown-wheel – and they both engaged with a single *'semicirculus'* – not with the normal two pallets on the verge.

The Latin texts offer far less detailed informa-

**6** Detail of an alternative form of verge escapement: the double escape-wheel engaging with a *'semicirculus'*, as used about 1330 in the St Albans Abbey Clock, based on Dr John North's transcription and interpretation of the manuscripts. This model was made in 1973 by Mr Peter Haward.

tion about the escapement of the going-train than any other part of the Wallingford clock, indicating no doubt that the writer thought it contained nothing new or unfamiliar to the average contemporary clockmaker. Although no other medieval clock is at present known to have had this form of the verge escapement, it seems possible that the double-wheel (or two escape-wheels) was the earlier of the two forms to be successfully used with a verge and foliot – unless it is assumed the two forms of escapement existed side by side early in the fourteenth century. Nowhere was it claimed that Richard of Wallingford was the inventor of the first 'horologe' and so it seems very likely that this form of verge escapement was the one in current use around AD 1300. Significantly, Leonardo da Vinci's drawings of horological mechanisms and other gear trains and pulley systems in the *Codex Atlanticus* (dated by Carlo Pedretti *c.* 1495) and in the more recently discovered *Codex Madrid I*, include several

drawings of precisely the same kind of escapement, apparently copied by Leonardo from some examples of medieval clockwork.

The earliest mechanical clocks of the Middle Ages probably struck a single stroke on the bell at the hour, just as many of the water-clocks in the Ancient World and in Islam had done, but at some unknown date 'hour-striking' (i.e. distinguishing each hour by a correct sequence of strokes on the bell) was invented. Indeed, Richard of Wallingford's clock has now been shown to have had an hour-striking mechanism – albeit fitted with a most unusual method of control – and the clock built for the chapel of the Ducal palace in Milan in 1335, the year before Richard's death, is unambiguously described as having one bell among several on which a big hammer struck a sequence of blows to correspond with the hours, beginning at one and continuing two for the second, three for the third, four for the fourth, and so on. Again, neither the inventor nor the place of this important discovery is known.

In Italy there are reliable records of striking clocks in 1353 (at Genoa) and in 1356 (at Bologna), whilst in England King Edward III's accounts include a payment of the expenses of three 'Lombards' (north Italians), one of whom is referred to as *magister orlogii* or 'master of the clock', for some six-and-a-half weeks in the spring and early summer of 1352, when the striking clock was being set up in 'the great tower' of Windsor Castle. There are also contemporary payments for a hammer, a pulley and a weight for this clock (*orlogium*). The bell for it was bought from Aldgate and the clock itself had to be transported from London.

The building accounts of other royal palaces during Edward III's reign (1327 – 77) show that between *c.* 1366 and 1370 three more striking clocks were set up at Westminster, the castle of Queensborough (on the Island of Sheppey) and the manor of King's Langley. The three bells alone were a major item of expenditure; together they weighed 13,228 lb and were paid for at the rate of 4d the lb. Furthermore, letters patent of safe conduct and protection were issued by Edward III in May 1368 to three named foreign 'orlogiers', one at least coming from Delft. The reputation of the Netherlands craftsmen in this new field seems to date from before 1330 when the papal court, then at Avignon, paid six gulden to a Master Nicholas of Brügge for a clock.

In these early medieval clocks and in their counterparts in the sixteenth century (*fig. 3*), the striking mechanism consisting of another set of wheels and barrel is a quite separate element, though it is released by the going-train of the clock. In the St Albans clock the striking-train and the going-train are arranged in parallel, but in most of these clocks the going-train was placed at the front and the mechanism of the striking-train was then put behind it to strike the hours from one to twelve, or, often, one to twenty-four. A separate weight provided the force for this striking-train, which was set in motion when a pin on one of the wheels of the 'going-train', upon reaching the hour, lifted a lever. The number of times that the bell is struck is regulated by the 'count-wheel' (or, as it is often miscalled, the 'locking-plate'), a wheel with notches cut in it at increasingly wide distances from each other. While the lever is held up by the count-wheel, the bell goes on being struck by the hammer. This simple count-wheel striking mechanism was not superseded for over three hundred years, when another invention, the 'rack-striking' device, was successfully applied to a clock by Edward Barlow working in London in 1676.

Although the clockmakers of the mid-fourteenth century had clearly mastered the problem of striking the hours in passing, the method of counting the hours varied from one part of Europe to another; there was no standard system until the eighteenth century. On Richard of Wallingford's clock, the bell was designed to divide the twenty-four hours into equal hours – not into the 'canonical' or unequal hours. Under the system of equal hours known as the *Italian Hours*, the count was designed to commence at sunset or, to be more precise, at the end of twilight (i.e. half an hour after sunset). Consequently, although sunset would always be shown as 24.00 on the clock, midnight, sunrise

and midday would change from day to day. Another system was that of 'canonical hours' whereby the periods of daylight and of darkness were each divided into twelve equal parts so that only at the equinoxes would a day-hour be equal to a night-hour. There were other variants, many of which necessitated the display of public notices laying down the dates on which an hour should be added or subtracted from the daylight period.

The Cassiobury Park clock (*figs. 2 – 3*), which was purchased by the Museum in 1964, has a fundamental form of construction which continued from the fourteenth to the end of the nineteenth century alongside the many new inventions, and it demonstrates most lucidly the simple open rectangular or 'four-poster' frame construction within which the mechanism is fitted. There is little about the design of the iron frame of the Cassiobury Park clock which helps to indicate the precise date of its creation. Its history is poorly recorded, but the manor of Cassiobury, formerly in the possession of St Alban's Abbey, was granted to Sir Richard Morison in 1546 after the Dissolution of the Monasteries, and the last great house at Cassiobury was built by the Earl of Essex in 1677. This clock has been in the house as long as could be remembered, but as yet no documentary evidence has been found to confirm its age or history.

A remarkable feature of the Cassiobury Park clock is that it bears an original mark; the mark is in the form of a cockleshell (about half an inch long), punched twice on the iron central cross-bar of the frame (*fig. 4*). The cockleshell, the very popular medieval symbol of St James of Compostella, may have been adopted by the iron master to mark the products of his foundry or, more probably, it may have been the clock-maker's own mark. The same punch-mark occurs on at least four other very similar iron 'turret' clocks, three of which originate from an area slightly north-east of St Albans. Of the three, the Quickswood clock and the Buntingford parish church clock both have inconclusive documentary references which suggest that they may be older than the seventeenth century, whilst the Orwell parish church clock can be traced back to 1610 and may have been made earlier. The fourth example, the Clandon Park Clock, is now in Surrey but the Onslow family may have taken it there from Hertfordshire in the seventeenth century or when rebuilding in 1731–5 the present house outside Guildford.

This small group of 'cockleshell' clocks cannot be reliably dated, though the makers of two related but unmarked turret clocks have recently been successfully identified. The more important of the two is the Rye church clock, which seems to be the work of a Gascon called Lewis Billiard in 1562, but the other clock at East Hendred in Oxfordshire was apparently made in 1525 by John Seymour of Wantage. The Dover Castle clock, perhaps the most similar, has no early documentation but when it was examined in 1851 by Admiral W.H. Smyth, Director of the Society of Antiquaries, and the clockmaker, Mr Vulliamy, it was said to bear the date '1348' and the mark ' $\mathcal{R}$ ' and the old Patents Office Museum subsequently confirmed that 'some miscreant a few years ago broke that portion of the iron from the clock on which the date was legibly cut and carried it off.' Few are prepared today to accept so early a dating for this turret clock but, of course, a date of '1548' would not seem in the least improbable and a rather indistinct '5' could easily have been read as a '3' in 1851. Since 1872, the clock has been available for study and display at the Science Museum, London. Very significantly, the mark ' $\mathcal{R}$ ' was recently found stamped on the Clandon Park clock as well as the cockleshell mark, thereby giving further weight to the 1851 report and linking the Dover Castle clock to the group of five cockleshell clocks.

The Cassiobury Park clock was probably designed to be wound every twenty-four hours and, like the rest of the group, to tell the time on a large dial on the exterior of the building, since the revolving dial attached to the front of the going-train appears to be a later addition and there are the remains of the 'lead-off' drive to an exterior dial. Fifteenth-century illuminated manuscripts show that, in Flanders and Italy at least, a twelve-hour dial (and a single hour

hand) was sometimes fixed on to the exterior of a building or tower. However, in the earlier period people probably relied on the sound of the bell being struck. Thus, at York there were ordinances concerning the regulation of workmen's hours; in 1352 the York masons took their time from the Minster's bells and in 1354 a bell weighing 55 lb was purchased to ring the hours for the workmen. These massively heavy clocks once called 'great clocks' but now more generally known as 'turret' or 'tower' clocks, were all constructed of wrought iron. It would seem that an early example designed to strike the quarters in passing was the famous Rouen clock of 1389.

The making of smaller clocks, suitable for use in a prince's household, seems to be slightly less well documented but there is, for example, an entry as early as 1337 recording that John of Engelbert, the chamberlain at the Papal Court in Avignon, purchased a timepiece for eleven gulden for the Pope's chamber; but these early examples have all been lost. One late medieval clock (fig. 7) is virtually a domestic version of the huge Cassiobury Park clock, and although it is designed to strike the hours in passing, it has a dial-plate and hand. The mechanism is fitted into the four-poster rectangular frame and consists of a going-train (with verge escapement with foliot) and a striking-train. The hammer, however, is pivoted outside the frame and swings outwards before striking the bell mounted above the frame. There is no alarum. The double-barrel winding system was probably intended to go for twenty-four hours when provided with a nine-foot drop. Pictorial representations in manuscripts indicate that this kind of clock was often placed high on the wall of one of the main rooms, but similar clocks are also depicted standing on a pedestal in the centre of a room, only a little above eye-level.

An early example of a 'clock' that was never intended to strike the hours in passing is the simple alarum clock (fig. 8). The mechanism has the verge escapement with foliot and is weight-driven, probably requiring winding every twelve hours. This clock, like so many of the small chamber clocks of the late Middle Ages, records the hours by the ingenious use of a

**7** Weight-driven domestic
iron clock of the late Middle
Ages with painted dial and
ornament below a pseudo-
architectural castellated
cresting. Probably made in
north-west Europe, but
conclusive evidence is
lacking. Height 20 in (51 cm).
*Presented by Mr and Mrs
Gilbert Edgar in 1967.*

**8** *centre*. Weight-driven alarum clock of the late Middle Ages, with a revolving painted wooden dial. Height 16 in (40.6 cm). *Presented by Mr and Mrs Gilbert Edgar in 1967.*

**9** *left*. A tarsia (wooden mosaic) panel from the choir of San Michele in Bosco, Bologna; executed by Fra Raffaele de Brescia between 1521–5 and depicting the sacristan's cupboard. *By courtesy of the Victoria and Albert Museum.*

**10** *right*. Detail of the tarsia panel (*fig. 9*) showing an alarum clock operating with a barrel (the earlier practice) instead of a pulley (as in the Museum's example, *fig. 8*).

circular dial that revolves. There is no hand; in its place there is a fixed pointer above the dial. The alarum is set by putting a peg in the appropriate hole in the dial and, because the dial revolves, the peg lifts the arm in front of the dial which releases the alarum mechanism. This type of clock was made to be fixed to the wall, though there is evidence that these clocks were sometimes fitted inside cupboards, if the artist of the tarsia (wooden mosaic) panel from the choir of San Michele in Bosco, Bologna, is to be believed (*fig. 9*). This panel, executed by Fra Raffaele da Brescia between 1521 and 1525, shows an alarum clock with a revolving dial (*fig. 10*), but fitted onto a slightly raised, square, open stand placed over a square hole through which the weights are suspended. Unexpectedly, the clock is placed sideways, probably to give easy access for winding; but if this cupboard

represents the sacristan's cupboard in the abbey church – and the objects in it are ecclesiastical – the need to see the dial and use it as a straightforward timepiece would probably be quite secondary. The primary function of the sacristan's clock was usually as an alarum in order to gather the monks together at regular hours for prayer. To keep the clock in a cupboard with an openwork lunette both enabled the alarum bell to be heard – at least by the sacristan, who could then have one of the big bells of the monastery rung – and at the same time protected the clock from thieves, interference and the gradual accumulation of dirt.

The Museum's alarum clock (*fig. 8*) is very similar to the one depicted in the Bolognese tarsia panel, but as yet there is neither reliable evidence to show where in Europe nor, indeed, precisely in which decade of the fifteenth or sixteenth centuries it was made. The clock in the tarsia panel from Bologna dated 1521–5 could have been made much earlier and have still been in use when the artist executed the tarsia panel. Certainly, an earlier dating would not clash with the evidence of the mechanism, in which one can see clearly the verge escapement controlled by the simple foliot, with its curving ends and its attached tiny weights designed to be slid along the foliot to adjust the speed of the turning motion backwards and forwards.

Throughout the late Middle Ages, contemporaneously with the manufacture of these clocks, clockmakers were creating similar timepieces in which the verge escapement was not controlled by a foliot but by a balance-wheel. The to and fro movement of the balance-wheel corresponds exactly to the action of the foliot but, once again, neither the inventor nor his place of work are known. The earliest record of the use of a balance-wheel to regulate a clock is contained in contemporary manuscript accounts of a clock made by Giovanni de' Dondi (1318 – 89), who devoted sixteen years of his leisure time while he was professor at the University of Padua to creating one of the greatest astronomical clocks of all time. He completed this clock in 1364, but detailed descriptions together with careful drawings (*fig. 11*) are all that now survive of this masterpiece. De' Dondi's astrarium was begun in 1348, twelve years after Richard of Wallingford's death, and it is interesting to compare the lives of these two men, whose brilliant application of the new invention of weight-driven mechanical time-keeping led to achievements that stand out far above anything produced by their contemporaries, so far as we know.

Giovanni de' Dondi was the son of the municipal physician of Chioggia, who had himself

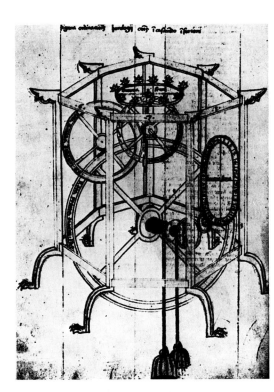

**11** A contemporary manuscript drawing of a clock made by Giovanni de'Dondi (1318–89) at Padua in northern Italy; completed in 1364, this clock incorporated the balance-wheel in place of the foliot. This is the earliest record of its use. *Bib. Capitolare Vescovile, Padua.*

**12** *far right*. Weight-driven domestic clock dated 1599 by Ulrich and Andreas Liechti, of Winthertur, Switzerland; it is inscribed on the side bar of the frame: 15 VAᐧL 99. The balance-wheel, just below the bell, is not a complete circle or 'crown' (as in the de'Dondi drawing, *fig. 11*) but has two segments removed – this rare refinement would have been introduced to improve the regulation. Height 15 in (38 cm). *Ilbert Collection; given by Mr Gilbert Edgar, C.B.E. in 1958.*

designed and constructed the astronomical clock in the Piazza dei Signori at Padua. Richard of Wallingford was the son of a blacksmith but, having lost his father when he was only ten, he was lucky when the Prior of Wallingford adopted him because of the signs of promise he already showed. As a result, he was able to study at Gloucester College, Oxford, for six years before entering the monastery of St Albans. Giovanni de 'Dondi was trained as a physician like his father but, significantly, when he was forty, he was a member of the faculties of medicine, astrology, philosophy and logic at the University of Padua. Unlike Richard, who had a very turbulent situation to administer when he became Abbot as well as the ever-worsening problems of his 'leprosy' and partial blindness, Giovanni appears to have 'with his own hand forged the said clock, all of brass and copper, without assistance from any other person, and did nothing else for sixteen years' (according to Philippe de Maisières, who knew him personally). Little wonder that he was able to win the patronage of the Duke of Milan, Gian Galeazzo Visconti; he died in Milan in 1389 at the age of seventy.

De' Dondi's astrarium was designed to display the motions of the five known planets according to the Ptolemaic theory, but in solving some of the associated problems he used elliptical wheels and, perhaps, the first known internally cut wheel, thus advancing the technology of clockmaking. Indeed, in his *Tractatus astarii*, he records many valuable details; for example, de 'Dondi's description of the balance-wheel, which beats two seconds, indicates that this was the normal rate of the common clock in those days, and he advises altering the weights attached to the balance-wheel if it needs regulating. One of the Museum's early examples of the use of the balance-wheel is dated 1599 and was made by two brothers, Ulrich and Andreas Liechti, clockmakers of Wintherthur in Switzerland (*fig. 12*). In this clock the four-poster frame is still remarkably Gothic in detail and, in the medieval tradition the wheels, particularly the larger ones, are still made as annular rings fitted to cruciform arms and fire-welded – not cut out

of flat metal. The mechanism of this clock is quite elaborate, being designed to strike both the hours and the half-hours in passing, function as an alarum clock and record the phases of the moon.

While many modest chamber clocks were being made, no doubt for rich merchants and townsfolk, a few immensely elaborate and grandiose clocks were designed for the courts of Europe. One of the finest of these princely commissions of the Renaissance is the magnificent carillon clock of Isaac Habrecht (*fig. 13*).

The richly and expertly engraved copper-gilt casing has been given a dignified and restrained architectural form in the Renaissance style. The six side panels, each incorporating a hinged door, are decorated with emblematical figures of the Virtues. Despite the high quality of the engraving and full-blooded Mannerist style of the ornamental designs, the name of the artist who was responsible for the ornamentation of the case is not known, though Tobias Stimmer, a compatriot of Habrecht, almost certainly played a major part. Isaac Habrecht himself may not have been personally involved in the decoration of the outer case but he was certainly responsible for the immensely complex series of mechanisms and dials.

The lowest stage shows a dial which revolves once a year and records the month, the day of the month, the Dominical Letter (which indicates the day of the week if the Dominical Letter for the year is known) and the saint's feast-day. The inner disc of this dial is engraved with the twelve signs of the zodiac in circles and the two pointers shaped like the sun and the moon indicate in which sign of the zodiac these two bodies are to be found at that precise moment. Through the aperture in the upper disc may be seen the phase of the moon and the pointer indicates the age of the moon.

On the second stage, seated on the pseudo-architectural ledge, are two silver putti, one carrying a sickle which he moves up and down, the other holding an hour-glass which he turns over as the hours are being struck. The silver dial between the putti records the quarters of the hour, with five-minute intervals marked out

**13** *far right*. The Habrecht Carillon Clock of 1589: a free, and relatively small weight-driven version of the great astronomical clock in Strasburg Cathedral, which the same maker, Isaac Habrecht, had created between 1571–4. This clock, with its architectural outer case in the Renaissance style, was apparently made for Pope Sixtus V and bears the inscription: ISAAC HABRECHT FABER AUTOMATARIVS ET CIVIS ARGENTORATENSIS 1589 (Isaac Habrecht, maker of automata and citizen of Strasbourg 1589).

After the Napoleonic Wars, this clock was no longer in Rome but had come to The Netherlands where it excited the interest of King William I (died 1844). In 1848, after its arrival in London, it was shown to the Fellows of the Royal Society. Height 5ft 2in (157.5 cm). *Bequeathed by Octavius Morgan in 1888.*

**15** *right above* View of the movement of the Habrecht Clock (seen from the right-hand side of the clock after part of the case had been removed) with the count-wheel of the hour striking-train in the lower right foreground; above, the automata and the carillon with its hammer levers arranged circularly around the horizontal pin-barrel and the bells placed above.

**14** *right below*. The four trains of the Habrecht Clock within a massive 'four-poster' frame but photographed out of its gilt-copper case; the going-train of the movement is on the left and the striking-train is on the right. Height 13½ in (34.3 cm).

between them. In the centre of this dial, there is engraved a map of the world. The larger dial immediately above has a normal hour hand, but it only revolves once every twenty-four hours, and not the usual twelve hours of the clocks in general use today.

The third and uppermost stage of the clock has four floors of automata. At the bottom, the days of the week in the guise of their planetary deities (e.g. Mars for Tuesday) in shining silver reliefs move round against the blue ground. On the floor above, a seated Madonna and Child in silver now accept the homage of angels who bow as they pass every hour, though originally the Three Magi were probably depicted presenting their gifts. The musical accompaniment for this procession is provided by the ten-bell carillon behind the casing (*fig. 15*). The next floor has four silver figures representing the Four Ages of Man; each in turn strikes one of the quarters, commencing with the little child and finishing with the old man just before the hour. The hour itself is struck by the silver figure of Death, on the topmost floor, whilst through the doorway on the left the figure of the Resurrected Christ, the *Salvator Mundi*, appears and reappears, as if to reassure mankind. At the very summit of the clock is a silver cock, which opens its wings towards the end of the carillon's tune and concludes the performance with a little noise – now produced by a pipe and bellows – which can scarcely be described as the crowing of a cock, though this was the original intention and was then achieved by a reed.

This very brief description gives some im-

**16** The Vallin carillon clock of 1598: this domestic or chamber weight-driven clock, shown with the metal sides removed, was made in London by Nicholas Vallin towards the end of Queen Elizabeth I's reign. In the truly Renaissance design of the case, Vallin has attempted to apply the principles of classical architecture, introducing a debased form of Doric column with entablature and pediment, and by creating an architectural perspective on the dial-plate he has added a unity of design.
Height 23 in (58.4 cm). *Ilbert Collection; given by Mr Gilbert Edgar, C.B.E. in 1959.*

pression of the complexity of this skilful intell-ectual toy which Isaac Habrecht had created in 1589, yet a closer look at the actual clockwork (*fig. 14*) reveals that the mechanism responsible for the measurement of time by this clock is basically no more complicated than in the Liechti clock (*fig. 12*). The Habrecht clock has since been converted from a balance-wheel to a pendulum, but the four trains are still fitted into a four-poster frame in the medieval tradition. The only significant modification is the placing of the wheels at right angles to the dial in order to solve the problem of winding from the side, which was obligatory in view of the elaborate system of fixed dials on the front of the clock and which was certainly not a new idea, even in 1589. Perhaps a more significant departure from the earlier medieval tradition is the use of brass for all the wheels in the four trains; furthermore, the wheels are cut from brass sheets, which in some cases had to be as much as a quarter of an inch thick, especially for the largest of the wheels.

Although the carillon chime is thought to have been first introduced with the turret clock at Aalst (in the Low Countries) in 1481, this Habrecht clock of more than one hundred years later is now the earliest surviving carillon clock designed on this relatively small – almost domestic – scale. Isaac Habrecht made one other version of this clock five years later in 1594, and this can still be seen in King Christian IV's 'Winter Room' at Rosenborg Castle in Copen-hagen among the Danish Royal collections.

Another remarkably early carillon clock, designed for indoor domestic use, is a London-made clock of 1598 (*fig. 16*). It was not, however, made by an English clockmaker but by a Flemish craftsman, Nicholas Vallin, who settled in London. The dial-plate of this steel clock is engraved: 'N. Vallin 1598'. Nicholas Vallin is thought to have come to England with his father, who emigrated from Flanders in the

**17** The movement of the Vallin carillon clock of 1598, showing the carillon levers placed in a straight line (on the left) and the pin-barrel mounted vertically.

1580s. The date of their arrival in London is uncertain, but in 1590 Nicholas married Elizabeth Rendtmeesters at Austin Friars, the Dutch Church in London. Unfortunately, he died in 1603 so that his working life among the clock-makers of London was probably no more than some fifteen years; four table-clocks and four watches from his hand have survived.

This piece is the only known chiming clock by Nicholas Vallin and is the only clock executed by him on this large scale (twenty-three inches high). It strikes the hours and, just before the hour, the carillon plays a tune on thirteen bells; at the quarters the carillon plays a short phrase and at the half hour it plays a slightly longer fragment of music. Unlike the Habrecht example, this barrel is pierced so that the pins can be placed to play different tunes. The construction of the Vallin carillon differs from that of the Habrecht, made only nine years earlier, in that the pin-barrel is mounted vertically and the levers for the hammers are placed in a straight line (*fig. 17*). In the Habrecht clock the barrel is mounted horizontally and the levers arranged in a circle around the barrel (*fig. 15*). These differences indicate that there were probably at least two distinct traditions for the construction of carillons. Vallin's use of two hands on the same dial to record the hour and the minutes is the earliest example in the Museum's collections with this feature, though in 1565 the Nuremberg guild laid down that a clock with a concentric minute hand should become part of the test-piece for admission as 'master'. However, the minute hand was not universally adopted in England, until after the introduction of the pendulum (*c.* 1660) because the degree of time-keeping was generally so poor that a single-handed clock showing the quarters was virtually as effective. It is perhaps a measure of Vallin's high standards of craftsmanship that he considered the meticulous introduction of a concentric minute hand worthwhile. Equally significant is his use of sheet metal – all the wheels are made of steel, cut from thick sheets. This break from the medieval tradition is in contrast to the rather conservative practice of the Liechti workshops, for example.

Vallin's clock of 1598 is one of the most outstanding examples of the improved method of constructing a weight-driven clock of the traditional medieval four-poster frame type. Although some clockmakers of the seventeenth century continued to make weight-driven clocks of the simple open frame construction, other makers had, since the fifteenth century, been developing a significant variant in which the four corner-posts were no longer held together by a narrow band at the top and bottom. Instead, they placed a thin sheet of iron or brass across both the top and the bottom. The top plate was pierced in two or three places to allow the verge arbor and the arm of the hammer to pass through; the hammer struck the inside of the bell mounted above the frame. As the hammer no longer swung outwards, the sides of the clock could be enclosed, and so create a neater-looking weight-driven clock that was, to some extent, dust-proof. The lower plate was pierced to allow the cords carrying the weights to pass through. In the early examples the technique of securing the plates to the four corner-posts (or pillars) was akin to the traditional method used for attaching the corner-pillars to the upper and lower narrow bands in the open-frame construction (i.e. by cutting slots and pinning). By the middle of the sixteenth century this technique had been improved upon and a threaded projection of the corner-posts passed through a circular hole in each of the four corners of the upper and lower plates, and was held firm by screwing a nut or an 'urn-shaped' finial on to the top of the corner-post and a ball-shaped foot on to the bottom of the post. The two plates were then held firm, like a sandwich, between the corner-posts and the finials and the feet.

Because of the high percentage of destruction of clocks of this period, it is now impossible to say whether Vallin's carillon clock would have been regarded as at all exceptional in his native Southern Netherlands, or whether any of his contemporaries in London (Bartholomew Newsam, Michael Nouwen, Randolf Bull, and Jacques Bulcke) might have produced similar clocks. Whatever the impact of Vallin's 1598 carillon clock on London's clockmakers may have been, today it stands out as a brilliant and quite exceptional piece.

A slightly later but far more typical example of a clock, constructed on the four-poster frame design with plate at top and bottom, is the brass or 'lantern' clock (*front cover*) signed by William Bowyer of London. This maker was active from the early 1620s until 1653, when, as Warden, he last attended the Clockmakers' Company. The Company had been formed under a royal charter granted by King Charles I on 22 August 1631 as a result of a petition from a large group of London clockmakers, who wanted to control the trade and its craftsmen in London and within a radius of ten miles. The training of apprentices and the number permitted to each master were supervised; in order to ensure a proper standard, the Company was empowered to search premises, by force if necessary, and no one was permitted to carry on the trade unless the Company had allowed them to join. Furthermore, immigrant makers had tended to dominate the London market and this was the second (but successful) attempt by the London craftsmen to establish a system of protection.

In the 1620s there were probably fewer than a hundred craftsmen working in the trade in London, but it was the time when the simple domestic brass clock, often called today the 'lantern' clock, was becoming increasingly popular with the merchant class and the business community; consequently the trade of making clocks (and watches) was expanding. The lantern clock was certainly to become the bread-and-butter line of the average clockmaker in seventeenth-century London – and there were plenty of rival versions being made on the Continent.

With the widespread introduction of the pendulum (*c.* 1660–70), these lantern clocks became even more popular both in England and abroad because of their improved accuracy (as is discussed in Chapter 4). Certainly the fashion for these clocks remained strong in London until the early eighteenth century, but in provincial centres – and for export purposes – these clocks continued to be made until about 1830. A revival in their popularity occurred long before the First World War, but those reproductions should be distinguished from the present-day spring-driven clocks fitted in the 'lantern'-type case. The true lantern clock was always weight-driven, and made so that the sides which box in the mechanism could be swung open.

**17a** The sixteenth century witnessed the debut of the 'watch' but, technically speaking, that story belongs to chapter three. This early German 'stackfreed' watch (see page 44), made by Hans Schniep, of Speyer, *c.* 1580–90, is neither light nor compact. Diameter 2⅞in (7.3 cm). *Ilbert Collection, 1958.*

# 2 Spring-driven 'Frame' Clocks

After the invention of the weight-driven mechanical clock, probably in the late thirteenth century, the next major mechanical innovation in clockwork was the use of a coiled spring to drive the mechanism. The first time that this application was successfully carried out is not known, but there is evidence to show that as early as the second quarter of the fifteenth century experiments with a spring-driven mechanism were being made in Italy by the Florentine architect Brunelleschi. The advantages of this motive force were very considerable, because while weights were needed, clocks could never be truly portable. For the same reason, table-clocks, instead of wall-clocks, became a practical proposition.

The change-over was not achieved, however, by simply substituting a spring for a weight, because a spring, when unwinding, exercises a decreasing force. If this changeable force were applied directly to the clock-train, it would cause the clock to gain greatly in the first hours and then lose heavily during the remaining hours. A device for equalising the motive power of the spring had to be invented before the spring could be successfully used in time-keeping.

One such device is called the 'fusee' (*fig. 18*). Nothing is known about its invention but its use in a 'military machine' dates from the early fifteenth century. The fusee is a metal truncated cone with a spiral groove cut on the surface. The spring is contained in a barrel, freely rotating on a fixed arbor. One end of a cord is attached to the barrel and the other to the base of the cone of the fusee; the cord is then wound on to the barrel by turning the arbor, and next wound on to the fusee from the barrel, thereby compressing the spring and creating tension. The clockwork is now fully wound and the cord is gradually pulled back on to the barrel from the top of the fusee, where it is at its narrowest. Consequently, when the power of the spring is at its greatest, it is transmitted through the minimum leverage; when the spring is almost fully unwound and its power is at its least, the leverage is at the maximum. A more efficient equalising device for this purpose could scarcely have been invented, and it is not surprising that it has remained in use, with certain types of escapements, until the present day.

The introduction and regular use in clockwork of the spring and the fusee before the last quarter of the fifteenth century is irrefutably established by the Latin manuscript notes of a clockmaker, Brother Paulus Almanus. This notebook, preserved in the City Library of Augsburg, was written in Rome between about 1475 and 1485 and contains the technical observations about various clocks that had interested this knowledgeable German lay-brother. Of the thirty clocks described in the manuscript many belonged to Cardinals, who were either visiting or resident in Rome; indeed, Almanus's description of the clock that belonged to Cardinal Hesler has been precisely dated between 21 January and 1 May 1480, when the Cardinal is recorded as being in Rome. John Leopold, in his definitive study of this manuscript, has pointed out that the writer, who describes as many as eight spring-driven clocks, did not comment upon them as if they were in any way unusual – indeed, Almanus frequently gives no more than a brief mention of the fusee. It would seem, therefore, that spring-driven clocks were no longer the exception among the rich, but whether all the eight examples described by Almanus had been imported into Italy from one of the leading centres of production in Bur-

**18** Diagram illustrating the fusee and the barrel.

gundy or Flanders (as Mr Leopold has deduced), or whether Almanus' omission of the names of their makers is coincidental and without any special significance, must remain an open question.

Tragically, fifteenth-century spring-driven clocks have almost totally disappeared, so that the brief written records and the occasional illustration in an illuminated manuscript or a painting are the chief remaining sources of information concerning these clocks, which are the result of a fundamental breakthrough and change in the method and technique of clockmaking. Most fortunately, one Flemish or Burgundian mid-fifteenth-century clock can be seen in London in the permanent display at the British Museum (*fig. 19*), to which it has been transferred on indefinite loan by the Victoria and Albert Museum; brought to London by a refugee family, it was given during World War II to the latter but without any record of its earlier history. Its significance only became apparent

**19** Late Gothic spring-driven clock, probably made in Burgundy or Flanders during the mid-fifteenth century. The dial, the bell and its canopy are lost but the surviving parts of the gilt-brass case testify to the high quality of the architectural design, with each column having a canopied niche containing a devotional figure supported on a slender cylindrical shaft; the bands of quatrefoil and lozenge patterns and the crocketted pinnacles are in the established Gothic manner. Despite its hexagonal form, the movement has a traditional 'frame' construction with plates above and below. Height 11¾ in (29.8 cm). *Transferred on indefinite loan by the Victoria and Albert Museum.*

**20** A reconstruction model of the movement of this Burgundian or Flemish hexagonal clock, based on an interpretation of the visible evidence of the remaining parts, of contemporary manuscripts and of the only other fifteenth-century clock with a spring-driven movement to have survived – the clock of Philip the Good, Duke of Burgundy (reigned 1419–67).

after lengthy periods of study in the British Museum's horological students' room because so much of the mechanism had been lost. Eventually it was possible to deduce what its original form had been and how it had functioned; a working model of the mechanism was constructed in metal and is now exhibited (*fig. 20*) alongside the remains of this once magnificent late Gothic hexagonal clock.

Part of the original mechanism survives and it is interesting to note that whereas the wheels (including the great wheel) are made of brass (cut from sheet metal), the rest of the movement is made of iron. Originally, the springs driving the going- and striking-trains were housed in barrels placed below the movement in a kind of sub-stage, and there are consequently two large rectangular holes cut in the bottom plate to allow the upper part of the spring-barrels to protrude. The clock was probably designed to go for twelve hours and it has been calculated that the great wheel in the going-train would have revolved once every two hours – slower than those in a weight-driven clock. The going-train has been constructed on the left and the striking-train on the right-hand side; the dial would consequently have had a right-angle drive. Indeed, seven out of the eight spring-driven clocks described by Almanus had right-angle drive for both the dial and the count-wheel. The advantage of right-angle drive in a spring-driven clock is the position of the capstans of the fusees: they are far more accessible and, therefore, far easier to wind.

The hexagonal form may have been uncommon but it was known to Almanus, who describes the Cardinal of Rouen's weight-driven clock as having six corner pillars and as 'beautiful'. The method of constructing a sub-stage area below the movement for the two spring-barrels only occurs for certain in one of the eight spring-driven clocks seen and described by Brother Paulus Almanus and may indicate that it was a refinement practised solely by clockmakers of a particular area. The advantage of this 'under-slung' method is that the spring-barrels can be reached more easily and even removed without dismantling the mechanism;

furthermore, the actual trains require less room without the barrels and the pillars and bars can be made shorter and hence more firm and rigid. Certainly the one surviving clock that belonged to Philip the Good, Duke of Burgundy (reigned 1419–67) has sub-stage spring barrels, and so provides confirmation that this was a method practised in Burgundy and Flanders. This famous clock of Philip the Good is preserved in the Germanische Nationalmuseum, Nuremberg, and although much of the exterior casing seems to have been replaced, the movement is mainly in its original state and is generally recognised as the earliest surviving spring-driven clock.

The sub-stage method of construction can be seen in a small spring-driven table-clock with both hour-striking and an alarum, which was purchased in 1973 in Switzerland (*fig. 21*). It has a very beautifully made steel movement in a four-poster frame with daintily fashioned corner pillars and an early, slim steel fusee. The gilt-brass case, which is designed to slide snugly around the movement as the latter is lowered from the top into the box-like form, is engraved on three sides with religious scenes from the Passion of Christ. The Crucifixion (on the back of the case) is indicative of the rather provincial quality of the decoration and a North German or Baltic origin in the middle of the sixteenth century seems highly probable. Three similar clocks signed by Steffen Brenner of Copenhagen (active *c.* 1550–1602), including one dated 1557 (in the Danish Clock Museum), have so many features in common with this clock that a tentative attribution to his workshop has been made. In 1550 Steffen Brenner received an annual salary from the Danish royal court and four years later was appointed court clockmaker to King Frederick II of Denmark.

The same kind of box-like case construction can be seen on another spring-driven, striking, table-clock, which may be of North German, Flemish or perhaps even English, mid-sixteenth century origin (*fig. 22*). Because the spring-barrels have been incorporated within the trains, the posted-frame has a solid horizontal base, and, as both the dial-plate and the extra

**21** Small spring-driven table-clock; the movement with its hour-striking train and alarum mechanism is shown alongside its engraved and gilded metal case. Made in northern Europe, perhaps in the workshop of Steffen Brenner of Copenhagen (active 1550–1602). Height of case 4¼ in (10.6 cm). *Purchased in 1973.*

**22** Spring-driven table-clock with two 'Jacks' (figures holding hammers) striking the bell at the hour; these two simple automata are attached to the hammer arbors of the clock mechanism. Made in north-west Europe, perhaps in England, about 1540–50. Height 12¼ in (31.1 cm). *Presented by Mr and Mrs Gilbert Edgar in 1967.*

horizontal plate at the top are part of the posted-frame, the movement is protected within a very robust and almost dust-free atmosphere once it has been lowered into its snugly fitting gilt-metal 'box'. The flat surfaces of the sides of the case provided an ideal area for engraved decoration; in this instance the mauresque or arabesque designs are typical of those created by Hans Holbein the Younger, who was working at the court of Henry VIII during his second stay in England from 1532–43, and those published in London by Thomas Geminus in 1548 under the title *Moryse and Damashin renewed and encreased, very profitable for Goldsmythes and Embroderars.* This is the earliest known book of engraved ornament published in England but it is little more than a pirated edition of the work of a French artist, Jacques Androuet Ducerceau.

During the second half of the sixteenth century the art of clock-making flourished throughout the area of German-speaking Central Europe but more especially in those city-republics, like Nuremberg, where the self-governing craft guilds set high standards both for the masters and for the training of apprentices. For some time the centre of European metalworking (from the mining and the extraction of the ore to the creation of the finest steel and brass) had been concentrated in Germany and, of course, the metalworkers developed skills and knowledge that were almost as essential as the raw material itself for the clockmaker. In Augsburg, the locksmiths of the early sixteenth century began to acquire the second qualification of a clockmaker, and gradually the clockmakers emerged from the all-embracing guild of the smiths. By 1564 they had established sole authority over decisions regarding their 'masterpieces' (submitted by each apprentice seeking to become a 'master') and the rules governing their craft training. For the next hundred years (*c.* 1550–1650), clockmaking in Germany was patronised by the rich, and some princes with true scientific interests encouraged horological works of great technical skill and artistic merit to be created. However, the very rigid rules of the guilds contributed towards the decline that

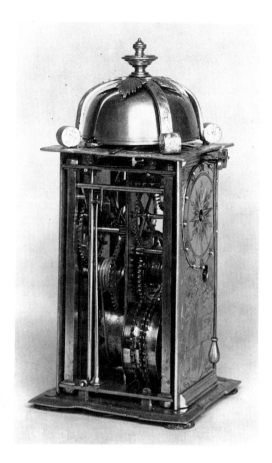

**23** *far left*. Spring-driven table-clock, with the sides removed to reveal the 'four-poster' frame with an extra plate at top and bottom, and the movement, which includes an hour-striking train and an alarum mechanism. On the back, another dial records the last hour struck – a new refinement that was needed when the mechanism was enclosed within a sturdy case that hid the count-wheel from view. German, second half of sixteenth century. Height 5⅞ in (15 cm). *Bequeathed by Octavius Morgan in 1888.*

**24** *left*. Miniature spring-driven clock in an enamelled, silver-gilt case; the upper dial with its hour-hand incorporates the alarum-setting ring, and the lower dial has the equivalent of a minute hand, but the dial is only marked with the quarters. On the back, a third dial records the last hour struck. German, late sixteenth century. Height 2½ in (6.3 cm). *Bequeathed by Octavius Morgan in 1888.*

**25** *right*. Astrolabic table-clock marked for use in latitude 51° (perhaps for use in Dresden); designed to go for thirty hours, this 'posted-framed', spring-driven movement incorporates alarum and striking mechanisms. The hour-striking train (for 1–12 or 1–24 as selected) has a subsidiary count-wheel for the 24-hour system – this exceptional feature may have been the practice of a Dresden workshop in the late sixteenth century. Height 13½ in (34.3 cm). *Ilbert Collection; given by Mr Gilbert Edgar, C.B.E. in 1959.*

can be seen creeping in by the middle of the seventeenth century, and there is little doubt that they led to a woeful degree of standardisation and repetitive design. With the trend towards increasing specialisation, clockmakers were tempted to sub-contract work and a form of mass-production of component parts grew up. It was not long before the contribution of the clockmakers in the German-speaking areas of Central Europe became less and less significant for the advancement of the craft and the pursuit of horology in general. Before the end of the seventeenth century the clockmakers of London had attained the pre-eminent position in Europe (as discussed in Chapter 4).

During this high period of clockmaking in the Germanic area from about 1550 to 1650, the spring-driven posted-frame table-clock was at its most popular and many have survived. A typical early example of this class dating from the middle of the sixteenth century may have been made in Innsbruck, where the workshop of Nikolaus Lanz was producing similar clocks. This truly portable striking clock (*fig. 23*) has an escapement, designed to be controlled by a balance, and was converted to pendulum, probably *c.* 1700. The steel movement has extra horizontal plates at top and bottom to hold the gilt-brass outer casing; the sides are simply pushed into place and held there by friction, for in these clocks the sides are never hinged as on the weight-driven examples.

Clocks of this type were obviously made in great numbers during the late sixteenth and early seventeenth centuries, but it is extremely rare to find a surviving spring-driven 'frame' clock that can be dated as early as the beginning of the sixteenth century. The evidence, therefore, suggests that these table-clocks became relatively more efficient timekeepers during the first half of the sixteenth century and their popularity caused them to be made on both a miniature and a monumental scale.

The tiny, elegantly enamelled version (*fig. 24*) is a fine example of German court craftsmanship about 1580. This silver-gilt clock, only 2½ in high indicates and strikes the hours and is also an alarum clock. On the upper part of the richly enamelled back is the dial for recording the last hour struck and, below it, an enamelled hunting scene with a deer, a hound and a huntsman standing with his hunting-spear raised but his head disguised within the antlered head of a stag. Each of the four panels of this silver-gilt clock has a different hunting-scene executed in bright enamel colours (light blue and red, green, black and dark blue) and, because of the extreme rarity of Renaissance silver engraved and enamelled in this manner, should be compared with that supreme achievement in this idiom: the silver-gilt writing-box with enamelled hunting-scenes by Hans and Elias Lencker, which was finished about 1585 and since 1598 has been recorded in the Inventories of the Bavarian ruling House, the Wittelsbachs (now in the Schatzkammer of the Residenz, Munich). Although the writing-box is decorated on a grander scale, the miniature clock has a similar quality in the style of the drawing, the lively gracefulness of the hunting scenes, the sophisticated Mannerism of the design of the dial-plate and in the technique of the enamelling. To make a clock in this tiny, jewel-like manner was in perfect accord with the Mannerist tastes of the Renaissance courts of Europe.

The clockmaker responsible for producing this miniature mechanism would certainly not have made the precious and highly decorative case – that would have been supplied by a goldsmith working, no doubt, to the measurements laid down by the clockmaker. This kind of teamwork would have existed among the craftsmen employed at any Renaissance court, but this division of labour also became the practice among the craftsmen in the German city-republics and, consequently, almost identical metal cases are to be found containing movements by different clockmakers from widely separated towns. Conversely, a German Renaissance clockmaker could – and did – purchase metal cases of very varied appearance to house his movements of almost identical size and design. Attributions on the basis of the exterior appearance of these metal clock-cases are, therefore, dangerous and only the distinguishing characteristics of the construction of the mechanisms provide a reliable set of criteria for identifying the work of the better known clockmakers. Unfortunately, many unsigned or unmarked movements have no immediately recognisable features or are still awaiting detailed study, so few of them can be reliably attributed to the workshop of a particular maker.

Among the anonymous German Renaissance spring-driven frame clocks in the Museum is a fine example of the astrolabic table-clock (*fig. 25*), so beloved of the Augsburg guild, when it laid down the original specifications for the 'masterpiece' in 1558 and again in 1577. Indeed, the 1577 rules remained in operation for at least 155 years, the details about the obligatory 'masterpieces' in 1732 showing no change, despite the journeymen's repeated petitions seeking to have the 'masterpiece' specifications updated. From the very beginning, the clock had to be 'about a span high', strike the hours and quarters, and 'the astrolabe runs as part of the clock'. In 1577 these requirements were amplified and, in addition to the geared astrolabe, the clock had to show the length of the days, the calendar, and the planets with their signs, as well as having an alarum mechanism and striking the hours both to twelve and to twenty-four as selected.

As a scientific instrument on its own, the astrolabe was clearly in considerable demand during the Renaissance, for it was essentially a

**26** The Polish *'grande sonnerie'* clock of 1648: the upper dial indicates the age and aspect of the moon, a revolving disc sets the alarum and the steel hand indicates the hours (I–XII), the quarters and the 5-minute intervals; the lower dial indicates the time according to the 24-hour system (in arabic numerals). The back has two dials: one to show the last hour struck, the other to show the last quarter struck; designed as a *'grande sonnerie'* clock, it strikes on three separate bells, two in the openwork cupola and one housed in the base with its own movement (*fig. 27*). At each quarter of the hour, the bell is struck – to be followed immediately by the last hour being struck again on a different sounding bell. When the next hour is reached, the fourth quarter useful and highly portable map of the heavens. Its rotating 'rete' carried representations of a number of important stars and of the ecliptic – the sun's path through the stars – whilst the stationary plate beneath carried indications of essential landmarks relating to the earth's surface. The astrolabe's usefulness was appreciated long before the Gothic invention of the mechanical clock, for it could be used to discover the times of the rising and setting of the sun and all the important stars at all seasons of the year, their altitude and azimuth at any given moment, or to calculate the time of day or night. Until mechanical timekeepers became truly reliable, the value of the astrolabe was considerable, though it was always dependent on a clear sky.

The application of geared clockwork to instruments representing the motions of celestial bodies goes back to Richard of Wallingford's great planetary clock at St Albans in 1327–36. The German Renaissance clockmakers' incorporation of the astrolabe into the more expensive, domestic-type clock presented no problems since the rotation of the rete over the stationary plate could be achieved without difficulty by mechanical means and could be made to move in apparent harmony with the stellar universe, rotating once every twenty-three hours and fifty-six minutes. The great effort and time spent in producing these clocks with elaborate astronomical and calendar information was of as little practical or economic value as the intricate ornamentation of the surface of the clock-case. These clocks were an expression of the age and, significantly, although their record as timekeepers shows them to have been both unreliable and inaccurate, they were clearly sought after as marvels of inventiveness and cherished as feats of mechanical engineering.

By the last quarter of the sixteenth century the more elaborate versions of this Germanic type of spring-driven posted-frame clock were beginning to be housed within the so-called 'tabernacle' case (*fig. 26*) with its two or even three-tier canopied structure tapering towards the finial and, below the cube, a spreading base, often deep enough to contain a subsidiary mechanism. One of the earliest and best documented examples of this tabernacle form can be seen in Dresden, where it has been since it entered the Elector of Saxony's collection in 1590, having been acquired by the Electress Sophia from a Nuremberg clockmaker whose 'masterpiece' it had been in 1587. A most ambitious tabernacle clock (*fig. 26*), dated 1648, may have been made for John Casimir, who succeeded his brother, Vladislaus IV, as King of Poland in that year, although when it was given to the Museum in 1867 by Octavius Morgan its earlier history had been completely lost and has only recently been pieced together from a number of different sources.

Now only 19 in (48.3 cm) high, this splendid clock was originally taller, for the canopy structure has been damaged and at least one

is struck, followed by the old hour on the second bell; the new hour would then be struck on the third bell. In addition, the alarum is sounded on the hour-bell. Height 19 in (48 cm). Made by Lucas Weydman in Cracow in 1648. *Given by Octavius Morgan in 1867.*

**27** *above.* The two movements of the Polish clock of 1648; on the left, the 'plated' spring-driven striking mechanism for sounding the 'new hour' after the last quarter and the 'old hour' have been struck; on the right, the 'frame' spring-driven trains, partially hidden behind the hinged pierced 'screens' (shown slightly open). Width of left-hand movement: 4 in (10.2 cm).

tier has been lost. The clock-case, made of gilt-copper, is skilfully and elaborately engraved and, in a most prominent position on the front plate, is inscribed in flowing script: *Lucas Weydman Cracaw A.D. 1648*. The immensely complicated mechanism is matched by the incredibly detailed decoration of the gilded exterior. Each side of the massive plinth is heavily engraved with scenes from the story of Adam and Eve in the Garden of Eden, together with a Latin verse commentary.

The sides of the clock demonstrate how concerned the maker of this clock was to create an all-round effect of sumptuous detail. From a technical or horological point of view, the sides of the clock could be plain blank walls but in this instance they have been transformed into windows of glass, through which, oddly enough, the inner mechanism *cannot* be seen. It cannot be seen because the movement (*fig. 27*) has been fitted with the most unusual pierced metal 'screens' composed of floral designs, gilded and minutely engraved, which are really created by an excessive elaboration of the usual hinged metal clips. These screens, when seen through the glass panels, give an effect of glittering, jewel-like richness, and, indeed, would be a quite meaningless extravagance unless seen. No other clock of this period is designed with *engraved* glass or rock-crystal panels; in every other case, the 'windows' are left clear, as on a very similar clock in the museum in Budapest.

The engraver of the glass panel (*fig. 28*) evidently knew that the keyhole had to be accommodated and so the inscription, SPLENDOR VANESCENS (at the top above the clouds) is no longer centrally placed. This alteration becomes even more apparent when the glass panel is compared with the source that appears to have been used by the glass engraver, a book, *Symbola divina et humana* by J. Tipotius, published in Prague in 1601–3, and again in 1642, six years before the clock was signed. The two emblems and their legends appear in precisely the same form, though entirely separate (*fig. 29*). The device of a bridge over a river was that of Nicolaus de Ponte, eighty-sixth Doge of Venice;

the other device, here stated to have been used by Leonora Malaspina, Marchioness of Terasana, shows two heads from the clouds blowing out the lighted candle – SPLENDOR VANESCENS. The only difference on the glass panel is that in conflating the two separate emblems into one composition, the legend 'Aliis inserviendo consumor' has been transferred from the top of the roundel to the plain strip on the bridge below the balustrade.

The choice of these particular devices to decorate a clock, which had obviously been carefully conceived and designed in every detail, may be related to the Polish King's death in 1648 which was widely mourned. The extinction of the candle, combined with the motto, *Splendor Vanescens*, could symbolise death; similarly, the bridge, in conjunction with the other motto, could also refer to the good king who had died in the service of his subjects. John Casimir may even have had this clock made in memory of his dead brother, for he (Casimir) had a very special interest in clocks, as is revealed by the inventory of his possessions made in France four years after his abdication, at the time of his death in 1672. His possessions were then sold in France, and, during a detailed examination of this clock, incised marks were found on the mechanism proving that it had remained in France at least from 1686–1836. Repaired on 6 June 1686 at Chantilly by a French clockmaker called Chrétien le Cadet, only fourteen years after John Casimir's death, the clock was subsequently repaired by a Parisian clockmaker, Gilles Bauve, on 24 June 1773; by La Motte in 1782 and 1790; and as late as 1838 another Parisian clockmaker, called Toutlemonde, repaired it. This clock was, therefore, in France for nearly two hundred years before coming to London, but whether it first reached France with John Casimir in 1668, when he abdicated, cannot yet be irrefutably established.

This magnificent clock is the work of many untraced craftsmen, from the man who cast the plinth with its lions at the four corners to the skilled artist who engraved the scenes of Adam and Eve, from the gifted clockmaker to the man who could engrave with a wheel on the glass

**28** Panel from the right-hand side of the Polish Clock of 1648, with its wheel-engraved glass incorporating into the design the keyhole for the alarum mechanism and pre-dating other surviving Polish wheel-engraved glass by some thirty years.

**29** Two devices from *Symbola divina et humana* by J. Tipotius (Prague, 1601–3 and 1642) which appear united on the glass panel (*fig. 28*).

panel. The other panel (on the left side) is a mid-nineteenth-century replacement copying, with minor alterations, the right-hand panel; unfortunately the wheel-engraved decoration of the original second panel of glass, if it was different, is now lost for ever. Indeed, the glass engraver may have been a Bohemian craftsman seeking work at the Polish court, for the earliest Polish wheel-engraved glass is said to date from '*c.* 1680'. Similarly, the clockmaker, Lucas Weydman, remains a shadowy figure and he, too, may have come from Prague, for in some technical respects the mechanism is akin to Bohemian clockwork. The links between Cracow, with its famous Jagellonian University, and the Imperial centres of Vienna and Prague had been long established; indeed, the earliest – and certainly the best documented – spring-driven 'plated' drum clock to have survived is the celebrated Polish Royal Clock of 1525, which was made by Jakob Zech, the leading clockmaker of Prague. Given to the Society of Antiquaries of London in 1808, this historic document has been miraculously well preserved, complete with its astronomical and astrological aspects, its thirty-hour movement and its foliot, the arms of which have threaded ends for the screw-on regulating weights that can be turned inwards or outwards for adjustment. This brilliant achievement of Jakob Zech is a landmark in the history of a fundamentally distinct and revolutionary method of clock-making to be discussed in the next chapter.

# 3 Spring-driven 'Plated' Clocks and Watches

At some time after the successful application of the spring as a motive force, probably before the middle of the fifteenth century, a totally different form of construction was adopted. In a Flemish or Burgundian illuminated manuscript, *L'Horloge de Sapience* (acquired about 1960 by the Bibliothèque Royale de Bruxelles M.S. IV, iii), written between about 1460 and 1480, there is probably the earliest known pictorial representation of this alternative form of clock construction (*fig. 30*). In this enlarged detail of part of one of the miniatures (folio 13$^V$) a clock is depicted without its outer case, thereby revealing beyond dispute its internal construction.

The movement is placed horizontally, and all the mechanism except the balance-wheel is contained between the two plates. Four pillars hold the two plates apart at the required distance but the plates have been used as a basis on which to build the mechanism. The wheels are pivoted in the plates, which in turn have become the bearing surfaces for the wheels and mechanism. In consequence, there is no longer a frame, a four-poster construction into which the mechanism is suspended and fixed (*fig. 31*). When a 'plated' clock is stripped down for cleaning, the plate is an integral part and has to be cleaned, whereas in the four-poster design the frame is unimportant to the mechanism and is left complete and erect after the clockwork has been dismantled.

Because the trains are no longer pivoted in the narrow bars within the four-poster frame, they could be compressed and laid out in curved lines, thereby using to the full the space available between the two plates, which could now be made circular, oval, rectangular and even triangular. Therefore, because the 'plated' form of construction has no vertical axis, and because a device was introduced by which the balance-wheel would continue to operate at whatever angle the mechanism was tilted, this new 'plated' form of construction was used for any timepiece required to function in an irregular and unpredictable position.

The great advantage of this 'plated' form of construction was that, as the clockmaker

**32** *right above*. Drum-clock with attachable alarum. The rock-crystal case reveals the working of the mechanism. Probably French, second half of sixteenth century. Height 6 in (15.2 cm). *Ilbert Collection; given by Mr Gilbert Edgar, C.B.E. in 1958.*

**33** *right below*. Detail of the movement from the rock-crystal drum clock (*fig. 32*), showing the going-train between the two plates held rigid by the three 'pillars' of steel, which are gilded, partly as a protection against rust and partly to be admired through the crystal casing.

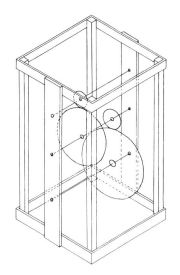

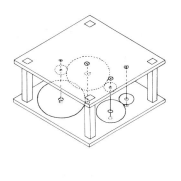

**30** *below.* Detail from a miniature in an illuminated manuscript, *L'Horologe de Sapience*, finished about 1460–80. This is the earliest pictorial representation of the 'plated' spring-driven movement – the alternative form of constructing a spring-driven mechanism that was to make possible the creation of timepieces so small that they could be 'worn', now called 'watches'. *By courtesy of the Bibliothèque Royale de Bruxelles* (MS.IV.111, f. 13).

**31** *top.* Diagram of the 'four-poster' frame and 'plated' clock constructions.

gradually learnt how to execute it on a very small scale, it could be used to create those miniature portable timepieces that could be worn on the person and which we call 'watches'.

The obvious disadvantage, initially, was that in the early horizontal 'plated' clocks the dial was placed above the movement, parallel to the upper plate, so it was difficult to read the time without actually getting close enough to the clock to look down on the dial. During the second half of the sixteenth century some movements were turned to a vertical position, mounted on a stand and so the 'monstrance' (or 'mirror') clocks came into fashion.

No example of a 'plated' clock as old as the manuscript illustration (*fig. 30*) has survived, but a hundred years later similar clocks were still being made and the example in a rock-crystal case is probably French (*fig. 32*).

This little clock, only 3¾ in in diameter, has a movement (*fig. 33*) that scarcely differs in one detail from the illuminated manuscript representation, except that in the latter the balance-wheel has not yet been fitted. The hour hand on the horizontal dial indicates the time, but the clock does not strike the hours. A separate alarum mechanism is provided, which may be superimposed on the dial so that a downward projecting lever is positioned above the hour at which the alarum is required to go off. The hour hand will, on reaching that hour, trip the lever and release the alarum. This separate attachable alarum must have been an extremely useful invention, especially when travelling.

Another early French example is an astrolabic clock (*fig. 34*), which is engraved with the date '1560' and, on the base of the drum-shaped lower part, bears an unidentified maker's mark, a Gothic 'M'. The 'plated' movement has a verge escapement with balance and a fusee; the latter may be one of the earliest extant uses of the so-called 'reversed fusee' – a refinement that winds the gut on to the fusee in the reverse direction and is normally to be found in late seventeenth- and eighteenth-century precision timekeepers. The movement is linked through the pillar to drive the dials on the front of the upper part. The front has a conventional astrolabe engraved on one side for use in latitude 48°, which indicates that the original owner may have lived in Le Mans, a major city in France, and, on the other side, it is engraved for use in latitude 51°32′, which might suggest that the owner also lived in the ancient German university town of Göttingen, north-east of Kassel. However, the elaborate calendar on the reverse, which is manually operated, is engraved with the months in French. On the pillar are marked out nine columns, one for each day of the week (in French) and the remaining two being marked 'Heures du jour' and 'Heures de la nuit'. The engraving collates a planet with each of the twelve hours of day and night; in the planetary columns the last three signs are repeated at the top of the next column to preserve continuity. Astrological information was, also, an important aspect of this type of Renaissance clock, and on the drum of this particular clock are engraved the signs of the Zodiac, each sign with its legendary figure, and on the horizontal surface, concentric circles representing the different celestial spheres.

Even the latter history of this exceptional clock is of special interest because, while it belonged to the gifted astronomer, James Ferguson (1710–76), he made an accurate detailed drawing and full description of it in his *Commonplace Book* (now preserved in the Edinburgh University Library). The drawing also faithfully records all but one of the later additions to the mechanically geared dials on the front of the upper part; the one omission from the drawing is the tiny black tidal dial in the centre – presumably because Ferguson had not added it at that time. As he seems to have received the clock as a present from the great clockmaker, Thomas Mudge (1714–94), the other eighteenth-century additions may indeed be the work of Mudge himself. Although this historic piece is always referred to as an 'astrolabic' clock, it should more correctly be called a 'timepiece' because it was never intended to strike in any way.

By the middle of the sixteenth century two very distinct methods of incorporating the

striking-train into a spring-driven 'plated' movement were in use. One method placed the striking-train below the going-train in a two-tier form of construction; sometimes the dial remained at the top in a horizontal position, though in France and Flanders the clockmakers modified this construction by placing the dial at the side (*fig. 35, left*, and *fig. 36*). The movement was still designed to slide into the case, just as in the crystal drum-clock (*fig. 32*), but the case was pierced at one point on the side to reveal the dial. Perhaps because of the need for a flat surface for the dial, these clocks were rarely cyclindrical, like the flat drum-

**34** *left*. The French astrolabic table-clock of 1560 marked for use in latitudes 48° (perhaps Le Mans) and, on the reverse, 51°32′ (perhaps Gottingen); the going-train in the drum-shaped base in a spring-driven 'plated' movement and drives the dials on the front of the upper part. Height 12 in (30.5 cm). Formerly belonging to the astronomer, James Ferguson (1710–76). *Bequeathed by Octavius Morgan in 1888.*

**37** *right*. Figure of Mars, from a set of engravings by the 'Master IB' and dated 1528; copied to decorate the French hexagonal clock (*fig. 35, left*). In the Department of Prints and Drawings, British Museum (British Museum [B.VIII 304.13]).
**38** *far right*. The movement of the Bartholomew Newsam clock (*fig. 35, right*) showing the two-tier construction in the French manner, though executed in a more sturdy fashion; the dial on this clock is a replacement.

**35** Two small table-clocks, spring-driven and hour-striking, outwardly resembling the proportions and general appearance of the contemporary German spring-driven 'frame' clocks (*see fig. 23*) but internally unrelated (*see figs. 36 and 38*). Hexagonal clock (*left*) made in France about 1530–50; height 6 9/10 in (17.5 cm). *Given by Mr H.J. Pfungst, F.S.A. in 1902.* Square clock (*right*) made in England before 1593 by Bartholomew Newsam; height 6½ in (16.5 cm). *Bequeathed by Octavius Morgan in 1888).*

**36** *centre.* The movement of the French hexagonal clock (*fig. 35, left*) showing the two-tier construction for the two trains and, above, the support for the bell which is normally hidden under the Italianate ribbed dome.

**39** Drum clock with an automaton figure that moves its arm as the hour is struck; the movement, incorporating the striking-train between the one pair of plates, is shown out of its case with its crowded hunting scenes executed in low relief. Made by Hans Gutbub in Strasbourg, late 16th century. Height 7¾ in (18.4 cm). *Bequeathed by Octavius Morgan in 1888.*

clocks, but usually hexagonal or square.

The Museum's collection includes one of the earliest examples to have survived; it is the copper-gilt clock engraved with the standing figures of Mars, Mercury, Jupiter, Venus and Saturn, after whom days of the week are named. This French clock is signed on the base: 'LOIS F.' but although nothing is known about this maker, it is unlikely to have been made many years after 1528, the year in which the engraver, 'IB', signed and dated his set of engravings of these figures (*fig. 37*). The engraver of the clock-case has copied them slavishly, but because of his lack of skill he has failed to recreate the subtlety and beauty of drawing that the 'Master IB' had achieved. Nevertheless, this piece, with its other decorative details borrowed from the repertoire of Renais-

sance ornament, is a delightful example.

These clocks of two-tier construction tend to remain less than 12 in high and so are always eminently portable. Although they seem to have been most popular in France and Flanders, at least two London clockmakers used this construction before the end of the sixteenth century. A truly splendid example is the clock signed by Bartholomew Newsam, who died in 1593 (*fig. 35, right* and *fig. 38*). The case and the two-tier plated movement are clearly based very closely on the Continental prototypes; unfortunately the dial is a modern replacement. Nothing is known about Bartholomew Newsam's origins or where he was trained, but he had attained the highest recognition as early as 1572, for he was then nominated to succeed Nicholas Urseau, Clockmaker to Queen Eliz-

**41** The 'Nef': a detail showing the tiny 'watch' dial, silver and enamelled, at the foot of the mainmast. Diameter 2⅜ in (6 cm); see fig. 17a for a contemporary German watch with similar dial.

abeth I, upon the latter's death. However, Urseau lived on until 1590 and Bartholomew Newsam only held that official position for three years before he himself died. He left some intriguing horological items, including a sundial for a pedestal, a chamber clock of five marks' value, a watch-clock in a purse and, most tantalising of all, a jewel with a watch in it. Clearly, he had not passed an unrewarding career in Elizabethan London, and although too little of his work has survived for a chronological development to be traced, this clock could as easily date from the 1570s as from the decade before his death, as is more often suggested.

The other method of incorporating the striking train was to combine it with the going-train within the one pair of plates, thereby retaining the low cylindrical or drum-shape form. An excellent version of this construction can be seen in a clock made by Hans Gutbub (*fig. 39*). The movement bears the signature HANS GUOT. BUOB, and the Strasbourg city mark is stamped on it. The maker has been identified with the Hans Gutbub who married Susanne, the eldest daughter of Isaac Habrecht, the maker of the Strasbourg Cathedral Clock and the two smaller versions in the Danish Royal Collection and in the British Museum (*figs. 13–15*). Susanne was born in 1569 and Hans Gutbub was granted *'le droit de bourgeoisie'* of Strasbourg on 11 February 1587, when Susanne was eighteen years old; it seems likely that the marriage took place soon after. Although Hans Gutbub was described as a clockmaker of Weinberg, near Bouxwiller, he clearly could produce work that was up to the high standards of the city of Strasbourg.

The highest standards and the greatest ingenuity were demanded of those craftsmen who sought the patronage of the Imperial court, but sadly many of their finest achievements are only known to us today from the written records. One of the most imaginative of the surviving court 'toys' is the large *nef* (or ship) containing a clock (*figs. 40–2*).

Underneath that grandiose gilt superstructure resembling a state galleon there is, surprisingly, only the same simple piece of clockwork,

**40** The *'Nef'* or Ship-Clock attributed to the Augsburg clockmaker, Hans Schlottheim. One of the spectacular automaton clocks of the Renaissance, probably made about 1580 for the Emperor Rudolf II, whose court was in Prague. Height 3 ft 3 in (99 cm). *Presented by Octavius Morgan in 1866.*

**42** The 'Nef': a detail of the movement with part of the adjacent bellows and some of the automata figures above.

be fired. At the same time, a kidney-shaped disc fitted at the stern on the starboard side lifted a corner of the ship up and then lowered it, simulating the rolling motion at sea. During this majestic progress, a fanfare would play on the small organ concealed below decks, activated by a pinwheel and blown by automatic bellows (*fig. 42*). Simultaneously the drummers and the trumpeters would start up as the Heralds and the Electors of the Holy Roman Emperor moved in procession before the Emperor. As they passed in front of the throne they would turn and bow to His Imperial Majesty who moved his head and the hand that holds the sceptre, as if in dignified acknowledgement.

A wonderful animated spectacle! But the maker of this *nef* has left no mark or signature on any part of it. However, there is little doubt that its creator was the Augsburg clockmaker, Hans Schlottheim (1547–1627), who worked extensively for the Emperor Rudolf II, who reigned from 1576 until 1612 and resided mainly in Prague. The written accounts indicate that Schlottheim had finished in 1581 a *nef* ordered by the Emperor, and his signed automaton with trumpeters (and organ) for Duke Wilhelm V of Bavaria, dated 1582 (in the Kunsthistorisches Museum, Vienna), has a mechanism that in part compares closely with the Museum's *nef*.

Of the many horizontal 'plated', spring-driven, striking clocks in the Museum, perhaps the most interesting from a horological point of view is the particularly beautiful square version with the famous Orpheus frieze running around the four sides of the case (*fig. 43*). This gilt-bronze cast band of finely chased reliefs depicts two scenes in a curiously misunderstood fashion; the well-known scene of Orpheus seated with his foot-lyre, and bewitching the animals, has been conflated with the scene of the retreat from Hades, but only Eurydice is represented coming past the three-headed Cerberus. If, as it seems, the cast reliefs are closely copied from the two engravings by the Nuremberg artist, Virgil Solis (died 1562), then in making the bronze reliefs, many minor changes have been introduced. These alterations are repeated on the nine other examples (mostly round) con-

spring-driven and incorporating the striking-train between the two plates (*fig. 42*). The only dial on this enormous ship-clock is so small (diameter 2⅜ in) that it is almost lost among the profusion of distracting detail. Both the hours and the quarters are indicated on this tiny dial, which is just like a typical German watch dial of this period (*see fig. 17a*). In contrast, the striking of the hours and the quarters was spectacularly performed by the little men standing in the two crows' nests on the mainmast, each of which contains an inverted bell. There is neither alarum nor any astronomical information offered, but an abundance of amusement. The ship was mounted on a wheeled carriage so that it could move along a table, propelled by its clockwork, which simultaneously caused its cannon in the bow to

taining 'plated' clock movements. Whereas all these cases seem to have originated in the same German workshop, perhaps at Nuremberg, there is less certainty about the movements. Indeed, as many as four different workshops may have been involved, for the mechanisms are constructed in widely differing ways. Whilst some seem related to South German clockwork, at least one has a mechanism that betrays many Italian characteristics. Significantly, the Museum's Orpheus clock is also designed for use in Italy, for it has a device that selected whether to have twelve-hour striking or six-hour striking (the latter being more relevant in Italy at that date).

Most exceptionally, it has a duration of eight days – an achievement rarely found before the second half of the seventeenth century. Furthermore, this Orpheus clock is unique in having an attachable alarum (on its four original, and exuberantly designed, supports), which is designed to go for eight days and after the alarum has been released is only able to ring for a limited period before it resets the trigger and so shuts off the alarum.

Another stage in the elaboration of the spring-driven 'plated' clock is glitteringly represented by a clock of 'jewel-box' appearance, resplendent in silver and gilt (*fig. 44*). The full-blooded Mannerist ornament, from the weird she-dragon feet to the pierced dolphin-arabesque covering the bell, suggests that this clock was designed during the first decades of the seventeenth century, probably in the Low Countries or possibly in Germany. Two different makers' marks were discovered during a detailed examination of the clock: one is a shield containing the initials 'AMW' (an unidentified mark that occurs on several clocks and watches), the other is 'BK 1612'. Only most exceptionally is the punch-mark of the maker accompanied by the date, and in this instance it may be read as evidence that the making of the movement had been sub-contracted to the unidentified maker, 'BK', in 1612 by the more established clockmaker, 'AMW', or, possibly, that the master 'AMW' left it unfinished for some reason and, after a gap, the less skilled 'BK' completed it in

**43** *left*. The square 'Orpheus' clock and attachable alarum: both movements are largely made of steel but a false impression of sumptuous expense has been created at the base of the clock by the anonymous maker, who has covered the back of the movement in a unique way with an ornately engraved gilded brass plate. Probably Southern German or perhaps North Italian, about 1570–80. 5¾ x 5¾ in (14.6 x 14.6 cm). *Bequeathed by Octavius Morgan in 1888.*

**44** *above*. Ornate square hour and quarter-striking clock, apparently the product of two unidentified makers; this clock was probably begun by 'AMW' and finished by his less skilled assistant 'BK' in 1612, working in the Low Countries. 7½ in square; height 8½ in (21.6 cm). *Ilbert Collection; given by Mr Gilbert Edgar, C.B.E. in 1958.* The movement of this clock is illustrated in fig. 53.

1612 without the guidance of the original maker, for the mechanism reveals two distinct levels of craftsmanship. The horizontal movement (*fig. 53*) lies in the square base of the clock and can be glimpsed through the windows on the four sides. The hours are indicated on the lower and larger dial revolving past a pointer, the dolphin that projects downwards from the side of the cylindrical upper tier. This upper tier contains the larger bell on which the hours are struck and hence the sides of the cylindrical drum are pierced, whilst above, under the little dome, is the smaller bell on which the quarters are struck. The figure standing on the dome revolves and with her long pointer indicates the minutes on the upper dial. One further refinement was provided by this clockmaker which can only rarely be found on clocks of this period: a detachable quadrant fitted into the base of the clock. The quadrant would have enabled the owner to ascertain the time from the sun's altitude and so set his clock going again at the correct time.

By contrast, the very rare English examples that have survived from the Elizabethan or early Stuart times seem to have cases of greater simplicity, none more so than the Museum's example (*fig. 45*), which is signed (on the back-plate of the movement) 'Robert Grinkin Londini'; it was purchased in 1981. Robert Grinkin junior (died 1661) was a member of the newly created Clockmakers' Company in London in 1632 and was twice Master (in 1648 and 1654). He had inherited both mathematical books and tools from his father, Robert Grinkin senior, when the latter died in 1626, and no doubt he took over his father's business, which was probably fairly successful since Robert Grinkin senior was one of the original sixteen petitioners seeking from King James I a charter to form their own Company of Clockmakers in 1622.

There is as yet no way of distinguishing between the works of the father and the son since they may have used the same form of signature. Unless one of their signed works can be shown to pre-date the death of Robert Grinkin senior, there is no certainty that it is not the work of the son. No signed work has

**45** Three English timepieces of the second quarter of 17th century. *Top right and left*: a square clock with hour-striking and alarum mechanisms, signed on the back-plate: *'Robert Grinkin, Londini'*. 4¾ x 4¾ cm (12 x 12 cm). *Purchased in 1981. Bottom right*: a gold watch and outer case, also signed *'Robert Grinkin, Londini'*. It was reputedly worn by Oliver Cromwell who gave it to Col. Nathaniel Rich, whose great-grandson, Sir Robert Rich, presented it in 1786. *Bottom left*: a watch with an alarum by David Ramsay. *Bequeathed by Octavius Morgan in 1888.*

**46** Six early watches *c.* 1550 – *c.* 1650. *Bottom left*: a German (perhaps Nuremberg) 'tambour' watch, with iron 'stackfreed' movement, shown below. *Top centre*: a striking watch signed *'Jaecques bulck(e)'*, perhaps English or Low Countries, with the movement shown below. *Top right*: English steel-cased watch, outer case of leather and *piqué* ornament, signed *'Richard Crayle fecit'*. *Bottom right*: English silver shell-shaped watch signed *'Jo. Willowe in Fleet Street'*. Width 1⅜ in (3.5 cm). *Right*: English striking and alarum watch with pierced floral case signed *'Sam. Shelton'* (died 1648). *Top left*: Swiss 'stackfreed' watch with striking mechanism made in Zug by Johann-Jakob Hediger for Beat Jakob Zurlauben (after 1649).

survived that can be securely attributed to the father.

This remarkably well-preserved table clock has a silver chapter-ring with Roman numerals and quarter-hour markings. It is designed to strike the hours in passing and also has an alarum-train. The silver alarum-disc inside the chapter-ring is delicately engraved with arabic numerals and a floral design. Both the hour hand and the alarum hand are made of blued steel.

Robert Grinkin junior had premises in Fleet Street, but from his very active workshop only a few examples (almost entirely watches) have survived to testify to his skills. One of the best-documented examples of his work – a very small watch, clearly designed to be worn – has been in the British Museum for almost two hundred years (*fig. 45*). The movement, with verge escapement and unsprung balance, is spring-driven with fusee and gut-line and has plates of gilt-brass, the back-plate being signed: '*Robert Grinkin Londini*'. This unadorned 'puritan' watch which was not designed to strike but does indicate the date of the month on the outer ring of the dial, was bequeathed in 1786 by Lieutenant General Sir Robert Rich, along with a portrait of Oliver Cromwell, the work of Robert Walker, *c.* 1649. According to Sir Robert Rich's Will, the 'small plain oval gold watch in a double case going upon catgut . . . usually worn by Oliver Cromwell' was presented to his great grandfather Nathaniel, a colonel in the Parliament Army. Nathaniel Rich was deprived of his command in 1655 and imprisoned for opposing Cromwell's government.

When Robert Grinkin senior wanted to take John Willow as an apprentice in 1609, it was done through the Blacksmiths' Company but after Willow was freed in 1617 he joined in 1622 those petitioning for a Clockmakers' Company of their own; he duly became Master only four years after the Charter had been granted in 1631. The Museum's watch by Willow has a brass movement within a silver case which has a hinged front and back, each in the form of a silver scallop shell (*fig. 46*). The dial is also made of silver with an engraved scene of Christ and Mary within the brass chapter-ring. The movement, a simple going-train with fusee, is signed: 'Jo. Willows in Fleetstreet'. His business, however, cannot have prospered, for the Company had to give charity to his widow from 1655–69; perhaps the Civil War was in part the cause.

One of the witnesses to the Will of Robert Grinkin in 1626 was a certain Richard Crayle, about whom little is known. The only known watch by this maker is almost entirely made of steel; it has a very well-made steel movement with fusee and fanciful 'barley-sugar' twisted pillars, 'worm' set-up and pinned cock (*fig. 46*). Not only the dial but also the case is made of polished steel. On the dial there is a revolving indicator between the chapter-ring and the date-ring and the signature on the back-plate reads: *Richard Crayle fecit*. Even the original outer case of leather and *piqué-point* has survived. This simple, modest, but very functional watch of slim proportions probably dates from the years of the Civil War (1642–6).

When King Charles I granted the Charter in 1631 and the Clockmakers' Company was duly formed, the first Master was the King's Clockmaker, David Ramsay; and an oval watch bears the signature: '*David Remsay Scotus Me Fecit*' (*fig. 45*). Born in Scotland and apparently trained in France, he was appointed Clockmaker to James I in 1613. His fortunes reached a low ebb under the Commonwealth and he used his position to obtain a grant from the funds of the Clockmakers' Company. He is recorded in 1653 living in Holborn and he died in 1660, too soon to benefit from the Restoration. Examples of his work are rare and the beautifully engraved gilt-brass case of the Museum's specimen indicates an early date, perhaps about 1620–30. The brass movement has a going-train (with setting-up ratchet wheel and click) and an alarum-train (with a pierced standing barrel) but no striking-train, for this watch was designed with a bell only as an 'alarum-watch' – not as a 'clock-watch'.

An early extant example of a striking-watch or 'clock-watch', thought to have been made in London, is the large, heavy round watch, complete with its pendant for suspension while being worn. It is signed on the back-plate of the movement 'Jaecques bulck[e]' (*fig. 46*). A clock-maker of this name is known to have repaired certain English royal clocks in 1599, but nothing else is known about his origins or his life, though it has been conjectured that he may have come from the Southern Netherlands like Nicholas Vallin. Although the style of engraving on the dial of this striking-watch is ultimately derived from French sixteenth-century sources, the flattened 'drum' shape, however, is as yet unrecorded among the very few extant French watches of the sixteenth century. The move-ment is entirely made of gilt-brass and blued steel; it has a verge escapement with fusee and a striking-train (for the hours) with a typical twelve-hour count-wheel. However, in common with so many of the late sixteenth- and early seventeenth-century watches, this one would have needed to be rewound more than once a day. Its steel ratchet set-up on the back-plate would probably have enabled its owner to regulate the watch both if it was 'gaining' or 'losing' time. The engraved border on the back plate seems to be more characteristic of very early English watches and is a feature rarely found on Continental examples of this period.

When and where the first watch was made is not known. It seems that no surviving example of a watch (that is, a mechanism designed to be worn on the person) can be dated before the second quarter of the sixteenth century, and all the written evidence discovered in support of a fifteenth-century origin in Italy or an early sixteenth-century origin in Nuremberg depends on the exact meaning attached to certain words, like *orologetto* as used by Bartolomeo Manfredi in a letter to the Marchese Ludovico Gonzaga in 1462.

Certainly by 1512 spring-driven timepieces small enough to carry in pouches (or purses) were being made in Nuremberg, but were they merely small drum-clocks (i.e. miniature table-clocks)? All that Johannes Cocleus wrote in 1512, in rather imprecise medieval Latin, was that in Nuremberg there was 'a young man named Peter Hele making objects which aston-ish the most learned mathematicians; out of a little iron, he makes timepieces [*horologia*] with very many wheels, which, without any weights and in any position, indicate and go for forty hours [*monstrat et pulsant xl horas*]'. Significantly, the city council of Nuremberg did not regard these portable spring-driven clocks referred to by Cocleus as worthy of inclusion in their customary presents to eminent foreigners until 1521. Then, between 1521 and 1525, no less than seven self-acting timepieces (*oralogia selbgeend*) – which can only mean spring-driven clocks – were sent to distinguished foreigners. At least one is stated to have a silver case but no doubt they were normally made of gilt-copper. On the strength of Cocleus' am-biguous sentence, 'Peter Hele' of Nuremberg has often been credited with the making of the first watch. This claim seems, at present, still incapable of proof.

A Nuremberg mathematician, Johann Neu-dorfer, published in 1546 an account of all the important artists and craftsmen who had lived in Nuremberg up to 1546/7. There is no mention of Peter Hele (or Peter Henlein), but under the name 'Andreas Henlein' he records briefly that 'this Henlein is nearly one of the first who contrived to make these small timepieces in musk balls . . .'.

As the Nuremberg archives record in 1524 the payment of sixteen florins to H. Henlein for one gilt musk-ball with a timepiece ('*fur 1 vergulten pysn Appfel fur all Ding mit einem Caiologium*'), at least one member of the Henlein family in Nuremberg was making a new type of min-iaturised clock, but he was evidently neither the only maker nor the first to do so.

A timepiece designed to work within a musk-ball may justly be classified as a 'watch' because it was presumably intended to be worn. Indeed, there is also the evidence of the Inventory of jewels given by King Henry VIII to Catherine Howard in 1540–41, for it lists a gold pomander 'wherein is a clocke'. These references of the 1540s together with the 1524 payment seem, therefore, to be the earliest mention of 'watches' in our sense of the word.

Regrettably, none of these references throw

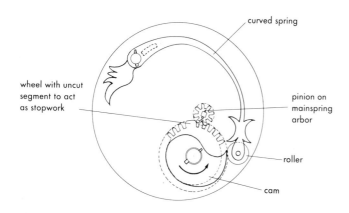

curved spring

wheel with uncut
segment to act
as stopwork

pinion on
mainspring
arbor

roller

cam

**47** Diagram of the
'stackfreed' (when the spring
is in the fully wound state).

any light on the mechanisms or their construction. Certainly the earliest surviving
watches fall into two distinct types, the spherical
version and the reduced 'drum-shaped' version.
The spherical form is extremely rare and perhaps the most famous is the French example
signed by Jacques de la Garde and dated 1551
(Musée du Louvre), the movement of which
incorporates a fusee.

The other type, with its flattened drum-shape
form and its pendant bar attached to the side of
the case at twelve o'clock and fitted with a ring,
is usually known as a 'tambour' watch. The
cases of the surviving examples are made of a
gilt brass (a copper alloy) and this design seems
to have remained in fashion in Germany for
about fifty years (c. 1540–90). A mid-sixteenth-
century example with a remarkably unaltered
steel movement (fig. 46) bears an unidentified
maker's punch-mark. It does not have a fusee;
instead, it has the German alternative device
for offsetting the variations in the force of the
spring – the 'stackfreed' (fig. 47). Neither the
origin of the word nor the inventor can be
traced, but although the device was rarely used

in clocks it was standard practice among early
watchmakers of German origin like Hans Grüber,
who became a master of the Nuremberg Guild
in 1552 and died in 1597. Its success in watchwork depended on the use of a long and rather
weak spring. It comprises a curved spring fixed
to the plate of the movement at one end, whilst
the other end has a roller that presses against a
snail-shaped cam fixed to the face of a toothed
wheel. The cam is located on the wheel in such
a position that when the watch is fully wound
the roller coincides with the highest part of the
cam. This device helps to equalise the pull of
the mainspring throughout its run and these
watches usually have a duration of sixteen to
twenty-four hours before rewinding.

A beautiful heavy German 'stackfreed' watch
with hour-striking mechanism and alarum (see
17a) bears the punched signature: 'HANS SCHNIEP
IN SPEIR' (on the back-plate near the edge outside
the free end of the stackfreed spring). On 10
June 1572 this maker purchased his 'Burger-
recht' or freedom of the City of Speyer on the
Rhine, and from 1572–99 his name appears in
the Lists of the Guild of Smiths; but in the next
List (1624) his name does not appear. A fully
signed watch in the form of a book by this
maker (preserved in the Musée du Louvre) is
dated 1583 and bears the punch-mark of Speyer,
stamped on the movement. A similar date may
be attributed to the Museum's watch, though
both the gently-domed convex lines of the case
and the silver and enamelled dial are of a type
that continued to be in fashion long after the
turn of the century.

The town of Zug in Switzerland is important
for the early history of Swiss watchmaking, and
the Museum possesses the only early watch of
indisputable Zug origin that can be closely
dated with certainty (fig. 46). The back of the
case is engraved with a coat of arms, crest and
mantling, surrounded by an inscription: 'BEAT.
ZUR. LAUBEN. LANDTSCRIBER. IN. FRIERN. EMPTER.' The
Zurlauben family was one of the most prominent
in Zug from the sixteenth to the eighteenth
century and bore this coat of arms. The watch
was apparently made for Beat Jakob Zurlauben
(1615–90) after 1649 when he became 'Land-

schreiber' but before 1668 when he became 'Statthalter'.

If the watch can be presumed to date from the years 1649 to 1668, then the partially obliterated signature on the movement can confidently be read as that of Johann-Jakob Hediger (1634–1718), whose family included at least one other watchmaker in the seventeenth/eighteenth centuries. No other signed work of this maker has yet been traced but it is significant that this Zug watch, which is designed to strike the hours, is in a number of respects strongly reminiscent of Nuremberg watches by makers like Michael Grüber in the early decades of the seventeenth century, and that it has the 'stackfeed' device in the German tradition.

Despite the successful and almost universal use of the stackfreed by watchmakers in the Germanic areas throughout this early period (c. 1550 – c. 1650), it was the fusee that continued to be the preferred solution of watchmakers elsewhere in Europe, particularly in France. However, their timekeeping qualities were probably of less importance to their aristocratic owners than their artistic merits as *objets d'art*. These watches were listed in the inventories along with the jewels – not the scientific instruments (if any). They were the new toy of the rich and worthy of being 'court presents' executed in exotic gold and gem-set cases, even set in a finger-ring, like the striking-watch made about 1585 and since 1632 preserved in the Schatzkammer of the Residenz in Munich. Such a *tour de force* within a finger-ring was likely to be the envy of princes and at each court craftsmen strove to create some new work of ingenuity and imagination. Of the eight watches listed among Queen Elizabeth I's jewels in 1587 perhaps the most curious was the *'watche of golde sett with small rubies small diamondes and small emerodes with a pearle in the topp called a Buckett, wanting two Rubies.'*

Five 'jewels' from among the Museum's collection of early watches (*fig. 48*) still contain their original movements, complete with signatures, and consequently provide valuable evidence both for the location and the dates of these centres of excellence. In France, a number of these finest craftsmen seem to have begun their careers in Blois (on the Loire) before moving to Paris. Under François I (reigned 1515–47) and the later Valois Kings, the French court began to spend much of its time in the Loire valley enjoying the hunt and other pleasures of the countryside during the day, and at night, music, drama and dancing in the great halls of the new Renaissance châteaux. The three-dimensional open cage-work of Louis Vautier's gold enamelled watch is so exceptional that it can be described as a unique survival. The surface of the gold case, painted with white enamel, is partly hidden by the intricate Mannerist pattern of the open cage-work, decorated with translucent enamels of different colours – a decorative scheme carried through onto the enamelled gold dial. It is just a timepiece with a typical going-train (verge escapement, fusee and gut) but the back-plate is signed: '*L. Vautyer à Blois*'. This maker, who was born in 1581 and married in 1617, probably made this watch around 1620 for a patron from the French court. Inevitably such expensive 'jewels' rarely survive, for as taste changes so their intrinsic value leads their owners to send them into the melting-pot so that they can be refashioned. Consequently, although Louis Vautier did not die until 1638, it is not surprising that so few examples of his work have survived.

A contemporary of Vautier in Blois was the maker Daniel Duduict, who is said to have been married there in 1604. However, he had moved to Paris by 1627 and his little watch with its exquisitely worked *basse-taille* enamelled gold case is signed (on the back-plate of the simple movement): '*Daniel Duduict à Paris*'. He died in Paris about ten years later, so this watch (*fig. 48*) with its floral design between the eight radiating bands probably dates from about 1630.

The same basic design, but using a totally different technique, decorates the much larger example, set with ten radiating bands (or 'spokes') each composed of eight graduated faceted garnets. In the centre, the large garnet in a very heavy setting is also faceted, but between the 'spokes' the floral design is achieved by a form of miniature painting in enamel

**48** Five watches designed to be worn as jewellery, *c. 1620 – c. 1670. Bottom right*: a French gold enamelled open cage-work case with a movement signed by Louis Vautier of Blois. *Bottom left*: a French gold enamelled watch signed *'Daniel Duduict à Paris'*. *Top left*: French (?) gold enamelled and gem-set pendant scent-bottle containing a watch (*see also fig. 49*). *Bottom centre*: a French diamond-set gold watch enamelled in relief with flowers, movement signed by Daniel Bouquet of London (active until 1662). Diameter 1¾ in (4.4 cm). *Top right*: English gold watch ornamented with rock-crystals and black and white enamel, signed *'Thomas Dyde, Londini'* (died 1686).

**49** View of the gold enamelled scent-bottle watch, showing the movement and the cover of the dial; made about 1635–50, perhaps in Henry Toutin's workshop in Paris. Height 2¼ in (5.7 cm). *Purchased in 1874.*

colours on the already fired white enamel ground.

This technique of enamelling was greatly developed soon after 1630 and, according to Félibien, writing in 1676, a goldsmith of Château-dun called Jean Toutin should be given the credit for its discovery. However, it now seems that the goldsmiths of Blois and nearby Château-dun were probably improving upon the earlier achievements of the long-established enamellers of Limoges (c. 1600), but that Jean Toutin (1578–1644) and his son, Henry, were among the foremost exponents of the new art.

On the evidence of the signed Henry Toutin gold enamelled locket in the Kunsthistorisches Museum in Vienna with its overall floral design on a white enamelled ground, this watch set with garnets (*fig. 48*) could be attributed to Henry Toutin's workshop about 1635–50. However, rival workshops imitating Henry Toutin's floral enamels may have quickly sprung up both inside France and beyond. Certainly, the movement of this watch is unlike most French watchwork, having neither a fusee nor the

Germanic stackfreed. It is simply fitted with 'stop-work'. By using a long mainspring, in which neither the fully wound nor the fully unwound state is permitted, the extremes of variation in pull are avoided and it is the stop-work that enables that section of the mainspring between the two extremes to be used to the exclusion of the rest. Because that middle section gives the most even pull, the best results are obtained – and in a purely decorative watch the timekeeping would probably have been more than adequate for the owner's needs. In this instance, the watch element was probably secondary to its role as a jewelled scent-bottle (*fig. 49*). The watch movement is literally encompassed within a tubular ring-shaped scent-bottle, complete with screw-top and two enamelled suspension loops on either side, so that it could be worn on a chain. None of its early history has been traced and its mid-seventeenth-century Blois or Paris origin remains to be proved, though the import of these luxury French watches with enamels on gold would seem to have been encouraged by wealthy English patrons.

The man perhaps most responsible for this type of import was David Bouquet, a Frenchman who was not only admitted into London's newly created Clockmakers' Company in 1632, but was Assistant in the Company until 1665. The records show that he made return visits to France and took French journeymen into his business in Blackfriars, where he worked until 1662. His most splendid extant watch (*fig. 48*) is signed 'D. Bouquet, Londini' on the back-plate of the movement, and is really indistinguishable from a French mechanism, with its going-train with fusee and gut. The case, however, is incontrovertibly French workmanship. The enamelling, both inside and out, is of the highest quality and, indeed, is a very rare example of the so-called Henry Toutin technique of enamelling in relief so that the flowers (petals and leaves) are raised up from the dark background enamel. In addition, the cover is richly ornamented with diamonds in their original thick gold settings. Even if David Bouquet made the movement, he had to import the

**50** Three watches with painted enamelled cases. *Bottom left*: watch signed 'Paul Viet, Blois', in a gold enamelled case attributed to Henry Toutin, *c.* 1640. Diameter 2$_3$<sub></sub>16 in (5.2 cm). *Right*: watch signed *'Blaise Foucher, Blois'* in a gold enamelled case with scenes of the Amazons. *Top left*: watch with balance-spring signed *Philippus van Ceulen, Hage* and enamelled case signed *I.L. Durant*, a painter in Geneva, *c.* 1680–90.

enamelled case and it seems most likely that the skilled task of mounting the diamonds would also have been done in the same Paris workshop, presumably to a special order from some English client who had commissioned this watch from David Bouquet.

Bouquet seems to have got off to an excellent start in London, for in 1622 he is listed as an alien journeyman at Mr Sampson's house in Blackfriars. This must refer to Sampson Shelton, an outstanding London watchmaker who became Warden when the Clockmakers' Company began in 1632 and was Master in 1634 and 1638. His brilliantly made watch with both striking and alarum (*fig. 46*) is signed: '*Sam Shelton*'. The dial incorporates an alarum disc within the silver chapter-ring as well as the outer date-ring in brass. The bell can be seen (and heard) through the delicately pierced gilt case with its finely engraved naturalistic flowers – a remarkably *avant-garde* achievement in case design. This type of case for striking watches became very popular during the second half of the seventeenth century, but this example must date from the 1640s because Sampson Shelton was dead by 1648.

French goldsmiths led by artists like Henry Toutin set a fashion for gold enamelled watch-cases that were veritable 'miniatures' – painted portraits, landscapes or figural scenes. Perhaps the most famous demonstration of Henry Toutin's art is the gold watch (Rijksmuseum, Amsterdam) with a movement signed by Antoine Mazurier of Paris, that was made for the marriage of William of Orange and Princess Mary of England in 1641, and which is enamelled with emblematic scenes and views of London and The Hague. The very similar palette and style of painting on the watch in the British Museum (*fig. 50*), with a movement signed 'Paul Viet, Blois', has led to the case being accepted as the work of Henry Toutin about 1640. The watchmaker Paul Viet died in 1656, but was already recorded in Blois as early as 1616.

The larger and even more splendidly decorated gold enamelled case of the watch with a movement signed 'Blaise Foucher, Blois' cannot be so convincingly attributed (*fig. 50*).

Blaise Foucher was active in Blois from 1631 until his death in 1662 but the artist of this unsigned *tour de force* in the new art of enamel miniature painting on gold remains elusive. This large case is exceptional because all four surfaces have been painted with figural scenes by one and the same hand, whereas it rapidly became the custom to give the decoration of the inside to some minor workshop assistant whose little landscape scenes on the inside rarely matched the quality of the exterior. On the Blaise Foucher watch, an artist of the highest calibre has been employed, but one has only to compare it with the signed and dated Henry Toutin locket of 1636 (in the British Museum – see my full catalogue entry in *Jewellery Through 7000 Years* (1976), no. 301) to realise that the former attribution to 'Toutin' is untenable, unless it be the sole surviving work of the father, Jean Toutin (1578–1644), none of whose work has been recognised. However, as the dial of this watch is executed in the new style normally associated with the second half of the seventeenth century, a date about 1640 for this watch would make it *avant-garde*.

A late and rather provincial example of the lingering taste for gem-set and enamelled watches in England is provided by the pretty little watch set with crystals and signed (on the back-plate) 'Thomas Dyde, Londini' (*fig. 48*). In its use of delicate black enamel on a white enamel ground, it is typical of so much English jewellery of the middle decades of the seventeenth century and it is surprising to learn that this highly productive maker, who died in 1686 at Enfield, was never actually a member of the Clockmakers' Company but, like several others, decided to remain aloof. The new Company clearly could not persuade all the members of the craft to fall in with their ideas and wishes.

# 4 The Revolution of the Pendulum and the Balance-Spring

Although many of the clocks so far discussed probably kept time sufficiently accurately for the contemporary civil requirements of the fifteenth to seventeenth centuries, the scientific mind had already begun before 1600 to demand a more precise timekeeping machine, both for astronomy and the associated problem of finding the longitude. An astronomer, mathematician and clockmaker from Switzerland, Jost Burgi (1552–1632) was working at Kassel for the Landgraf Wilhelm IV of Hesse when in about 1590 he introduced into clockwork a new form of escapement, the 'cross-beat'. It was a type of double verge; in place of the vertical verge with two pallets or 'flags' (*see fig. 1*), Burgi designed two arbors (each with one pallet) geared or meshing with each other in the middle, whilst each end was fitted with adjustable 'wings' or balance-arms. In common with the verge escapement, one pallet is always in a position to receive an impulse as soon as a tooth has 'escaped' from the other pallet. Since the arbors are geared together, the action of a tooth on either pallet will cause both foliots to move slowly in opposed directions.

Burgi's new escapement did not become widely known and very few examples either by his own hand or by his followers survive; in the Museum's collection the best-preserved version is a weight-driven timepiece (*fig. 51*) inscribed (on the dial) 'Arnstad', presumably made by a clockmaker of that town which lies to the east of Kassel.

Although the cross-beat escapement enabled Burgi to achieve far more accurate timekeeping, his invention of the remontoire – an automatic device which adjusts the drive-force so that it is transmitted at a constant level – was a vast improvement on the fusee (*fig. 18*). In 1981 (with funds from the British Museum Society) a unique example, made about 1600 in some Germanic centre such as Vienna or Augsburg, was acquired (*fig. 52*). It appears to be the only known Renaissance clock mechanism designed to strike the half-quarters (every 7½ minutes) as well as the hours and the quarters. The four main trains are driven by the one large spring-barrel, positioned in the sub-stage area below

the mechanism, and, in order to supply an even force, the maker has introduced the remontoire into the going-train; because he linked it to the striking-train, the remontoire is rewound every 7½ minutes. This is the only example to have survived and is a brilliant feat, for this maker has achieved a rewinding of the remontoire twice as frequently as had been achieved by the most sophisticated of Brugi's surviving clocks with remontoires. The more frequently the remontoire is rewound, the fewer the errors transmitted to the escapement. In 1664 Christian Huygens in Holland achieved a rewind of the remontoire every half-minute, and in England John Harrison (in 1761) achieved a rewind every 7½ seconds. Finally, in 1774, Thomas Mudge rewound the remontoire on each beat of the balance (i.e. five times every second). Such a degree of technical accuracy led Mudge's invention to become known as the 'constant force escapement'.

The combination of both remontoire and cross-beat escapement was incorporated in an unsigned clock purchased by the Museum in 1973 and now attributed to Hans Buschmann of Augsburg (*c.* 1630–50). Although the spring-driven movement is very incomplete, it is a most interesting and valuable document.

Jost Burgi died in 1632 and within twenty-five years his great technical achievements were eclipsed by that revolutionary invention, the pendulum, which was successfully applied as a regulator of clockwork in 1657. In that year Salomon Coster, a clockmaker working in The Hague for the famous Dutch astronomer and mathematician, Christian Huygens, appears to have been the first to construct a fully-fledged

pendulum clock. In the following year Huygens published the first accurate treatise on the pendulum and incorporated a detailed design for a pendulum clock.

The pendulum has inherent timekeeping properties because it is restored by gravity. Whereas the foliot and balance will remain in whatever position they may be when they come to rest, the pendulum will always come to rest in the one position, the point in the arc where the pendulum bob is at its lowest, because of the force of gravity. By successfully applying a clock mechanism to keep the pendulum swinging, to count its swings and translate them into hours and minutes on the dial, Christian Huygens made possible the production of clocks that were far more consistent timekeepers. Because the pendulum is subject to the physical law of gravity, it, unlike the foliot and balance, is less dependent on variations in force within the clockwork.

Nevertheless, there remained a degree of inaccuracy so large that it continued to offer a challenge to clockmakers and scientists of succeeding generations. These inaccuracies arose largely from the imperfections in the methods used to maintain the pendulum in motion.

Although Christian Huygens designed the pendulum for a weight-driven clock, his clockmaker, Saloman Coster, soon produced a spring-driven clock with pendulum in place of a balance. The type of movement he used was only a slight modification of the standard spring-driven table-clock movement (*fig. 53*), but, of course, it could no longer remain horizontal because of the pendulum. This method of construction, in a slightly modified form, was used by the great majority of European clockmakers to produce the standard type of 'plated' movement which has remained in demand until the present day (*fig. 31*).

The most celebrated of early English makers, Edward East (1602–96), made vertical table-clocks (often called 'bracket-clocks') of this construction, and one of his very early examples, probably dates from the beginning of the 1660s (*figs. 54, 55*). As so often in the first ten years following a new invention in clockmaking, the

**53.** Movement of the 1612 table-clock (*fig. 44*), which is typical of the spring-driven, 'plated' movements in the standard horizontal clocks, placed in a vertical position in order to compare with fig. 54.

**54** *right*. Movement of the tableclock in fig. 55, showing a typical spring-driven 'plated' clock with pendulum. Height of back-plate 8¾ in (22.2 cm).

**57** Movement of the long-case clock by Ahasuerus Fromanteel (see Contents page); weight-driven with short pendulum. Height of back-plate 7¾ in (19.7 cm).

exterior appearance of the clock is extremely simple and austere. No attempt to disguise the shallow rectangular form of the 'plated' construction has been made. The movement and dial-plate are placed in a wooden, box-like case, with glass panels in the sides and in the front, the latter being hinged for access to the key-holes for winding. This eight-day clock strikes the hours and has a conventional verge escapement.

Less stark and functional is the 'architectural' case (*fig. 56*), in which a movement signed by Henry Jones repeats all the features of the Edward East. This maker, who rose to an eminent position, had been apprenticed to Edward East in 1654. He was appointed Assistant in the Company from 1676, having only three years before complained that his name had

**55** *right*. Table-clock (often called a bracket clock) by Edward East about 1660. Its sober outer appearance is odd and in striking contrast to the tastes of the court of Charles II and Restoration England, especially when it is remembered that as early as November 1660 Edward East had been appointed Chief Clockmaker to King Charles II. Height 14¼ in (36.2 cm). *Ilbert Collection; given by Mr Gilbert Edgar C.B.E. in 1958.*

been erased from a royal clock. After his year as Master in 1691, he gave the Company £100 for the poor. When he died in 1695 he was only about fifty-three years old.

When the pendulum was applied to weight-driven clocks. the same method of construction was used but the sequence of development which has been traced in 'frame' clock practice was reversed; the barrel for the weights replaced the fusee. This can be seen very clearly in the movement (*fig. 57*) of the eight-day long-case ('grandfather') clock by Ahasuerus Fromanteel (1607–93); this movement has the conventional verge escapement. Although this clock has the short bob pendulum, nevertheless it is fitted into a long-case 6ft 4in high, because of the weights – either to protect or to hide them (*see inside back cover*). In this clock, Fromanteel, who is famous for bringing to England in 1658 his first-hand knowledge of the Dutch experiments and final discovery of how to construct a true pendulum clock, has also introduced a calendar on the dial-plate. Ahasuerus Fromanteel has signed his name on the dial-plate below the chapter-ring at six o'clock; conse-

quently it cannot be read when the hood is in position. In order to wind this clock, the hood has to be lifted. This is a clumsy design that remained fairly common in England until the end of the seventeenth century.

The most common English weight-driven clock before the invention of the pendulum clock was the simple brass 'lantern' clock, like the one by William Bowyer (*see front cover and p.19*). With slight modifications, the pendulum was applied to these 'lantern' clocks, as can be seen on the British Museum's example by Daniel Quare and made in London about 1670. The Dutch also favoured this type of clock, and one late seventeenth-century example is particularly impressive (*see front cover*). The massive three-train brass movement needs winding every thirty hours, and the 'frame' has the distinctive twisted columns of those grandiose Dutch 'posted-frame' clocks often attributed to Groningen. In addition, this clock has so-called 'Dutch striking', by which the hour is struck in passing and is repeated on a higher tone bell at the half-hour. It has a concentric minute hand and its original cast hour hand incorporates the alarum-setting dial. Below the chapter-ring there is a calendar aperture for the date of the month, while above, a lunar dial shows the phases of the moon. The pierced cresting is cast, and on the front section the cartouche is engraved with a four-line moralising inscription in Dutch. Few English lantern clocks could rival this elaborate version from Holland.

In 1675 the Dutch astronomer Christian Huygens once again made history when he published his claim to the invention of the balance-spring, a solution that was as revolutionary for watch-making as the pendulum was to clockmaking. By successfully applying a spring to control the balance, Huygens offered an alternative means of regulating the timekeeping without making any change to the actual driving force of the timepiece. Although Huygens's claim was immediately challenged by an Englishman, Robert Hooke, who claimed to have originated the same solution some fifteen years before, nevertheless it was Christian Huygens who in 1675 had applied the spring in its successful spiral

**56** *below.* Table-clock with eight-day movement with a verge escapement and short pendulum; hour-striking; signed *'Henry Jones in the Temple'.* Made in London about 1675. Height 25 in (63.5 cm). *Bequeathed by Mr C.A.W. Boothroyd in 1978.*

**63** An Italian Night-Clock, designed to be read in the dark from a distance and containing an almost entirely silent movement by Pietro Campani, who made it in Rome in 1683. height 3 ft 3 in (99 cm). *Ilbert Collection; given by Mr Gilbert Edgar, C.B.E. in 1958.*

**58** Two English watches made about 1675–80). *Left*: a watch with verge and fusee movement; on the back-plate a seconds-dial (the hand revolving anti-clockwise); signed *'Charles Gretton, London'*. Diameter 2¼ in (5.7 cm). *Right*: a watch with balance-spring and with a seconds dial signed *'Tho. Tompion London No. 4'*. Diameter 2 1/16 in (5.2 cm). *Both from the Ilbert Collection*.

form. Although experiments using straight springs had undoubtedly begun in the 1660s and Hooke could claim that he had commissioned Thomas Tompion to make him a watch with a balance-spring, the dispute was never finally settled. Certainly, Tompion was making watches with balance-springs soon after 1675 and one of his earliest achievements is signed on the back-plate 'Tho Tompion London No. 4' (*fig. 58, right*). The movement, with its verge escapement and fusee, is controlled by a spiral balance-spring, and on the dial there is a subsidiary tiny dial with a seconds hand.

Prior to the successful application of the balance-spring to watchwork, the poor time-keeping of most watches had scarcely justified the extra work of a concentric minute hand. Indeed, few watches with minute hands pre-date the introduction of the balance-spring, but one remarkable exception is illustrated next to Tompion's 'No.4'. The movement (*fig. 58, left*) is signed 'Charles Gretton London' and has a going-train with verge escapement and fusee and an 'endless screw' setting-up device. However, in addition to the concentric minute hand on the main dial, Gretton has most exceptionally introduced (on the back-plate) a tiny subsidiary seconds dial with a seconds hand. Since Charles Gretton only completed his apprenticeship and was 'free' of the Company in 1672, this watch

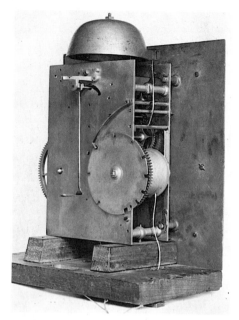

**60** *far left*. Movement of the long-case clock by Joseph Knibb (*see inside back cover*), showing the count-wheel and, at the top of the back-plate, the pallet arbor and crutch supported by the back-cock, from which the normal long 'seconds' pendulum is suspended (but removed in this photograph). Height of back-plate 7½ in (19 cm).

**61** *left*. Detail of the movement by Joseph Knibb (*see fig. 60*), showing the escapewheel and the pallet – an early example of the 'anchor' escapement.

**59** Diagram of the 'anchor' escapement.

must have been made in London at approximately the same time as Christian Huygens was getting ready to publish his invention of the balance-spring. Consequently, there are probably fewer than ten years between the dates of these two watches and, although Tompion's incorporates the spiral balance-spring, their outward appearance is almost the same – even their outer cases are both made of the fashionable tortoiseshell decorated with silver *piqué*.

On the Continent, watch movements with balance-springs were frequently fitted with painted enamel cases supplied by the very active workshops in Geneva, where a flourishing school of enamelling in the tradition of the French (Blois and Paris) centres grew up in the last quarter of the seventeenth century. The Huaud family of enamellers in Geneva were the most prolific and exported their cases to watchmakers throughout Europe, but a greater rarity is the excellent watch by Philippus van Ceulen of The Hague which is in a case signed 'I.L. Durant pinx' (*fig. 50*). This artist signed a beautiful portrait miniature dated 1681 (in the Geneva Museum) and is recorded as an enamel

painter in the Geneva State archives for 1685. His style of painting and the rare tonal quality of his enamels typifies the best in Swiss enamelling in the last decades of the seventeenth century.

Whereas Charles Gretton went on to build a prosperous business in Fleet Street, becoming Master of the Company in 1700, Thomas Tompion became a household name and unquestionably the best known of English clockmakers abroad. Yet his origins are obscure and nothing is known of his apprenticeship. The first record of his presence in London seems to date from 1671 (when he was thirty-two years old), and in that year the Company made him a Free Brother. His rise to a position of eminence was remarkably swift, as the Museum's collection of his work serves to illustrate quite dramatically.

Tompion, and the two 'Great Clocks' he made in 1675–6 for the Royal Observatory (*see Figs. 67, 69*) are at the very beginning of the long story of how Greenwich Time eventually became Universal Time all over the world and not, for example, Nuremberg time or Paris time. Charles II had established the Greenwich Observatory in 1675 to assist studies in astronomy for the benefit of navigation and had appointed John Flamsteed as his 'Astronomer Royal'. Flamsteed's patron, Sir Jonas Moore, immediately arranged for Thomas Tompion to make these two clocks, the design of which had been so carefully calculated to include special features that it would make them the most accurate clocks in the world. After much effort, Tompion produced a clock (*see fig. 67*) that goes for a year without being rewound, has a pendulum 13 ft long suspended *above* the movement and beating every two seconds, and thirdly, an escapement that was even an advance on London's very latest achievement – the anchor (or recoil) escapement of the early 1670s (*fig. 59*).

The benefits of Huygens's application of the pendulum in 1657 had been limited because the clockmakers were still using the verge escapement, with all its inadequacies. So in an attempt to reduce the swing of the pendulum one of the leading pioneers in London, probably Joseph Knibb, but perhaps Robert Hooke or William Clements, created an escapement that now always referred to as the anchor escapement (*fig. 59*). The anchor is indirectly attached to the pendulum and as a tooth of the 'scape-wheel escapes from the pallet at one end of the anchor, so a tooth on the other side engages with the pallet at the opposite end of the anchor. This repetitive action is motivated by the driving force of the clockwork, and it was found that this enabled the arc of the pendulum to be greatly reduced. An early example of the application of this escapement is the elegant long-case clock by Joseph Knibb of London (*see inside back cover*). The weights hang down inside the 6ft 4in-high case of ebonised pearwood, and the subdued gilded dial-plate with its silvered chapter-ring is protected under the hood of classical design. This view of the movement (*fig. 60*) shows the back-cock which supports the pallet arbor and crutch and on which the pendulum is hung. In this view the pendulum has been removed, but it would have hung down and been lightly engaged by the fork at the lower end of the crutch. The pendulum, which beats seconds, is just over 39 in long, the standard length for a seconds pendulum. In this detail (*fig. 61*) taken from the other side of the movement, the 'scape-wheel and the anchor are plainly visible. Joseph Knibb (1640–1711) was one of the most skilful of London makers but only became a Free Brother of the Company in 1670 when he had left Oxford and settled in London. He probably made this clock, which strikes the hours, in the late 1670s.

Made about the same time, soon after 1680, is a remarkably unspoilt clock by Tompion (*see contents page*). The movement has the anchor escapement, like the Knibb, but whereas Knibb's clock is an eight-day clock, Tompion's movement will go for a month. In addition, Tompion has fitted a calendar aperture in the dial, giving both the days of the week and the months of the year, and (below) his signature is engraved: 'Tho. Tompion, Londini, fecit'. This movement is also an early example of the application of another new invention – the so-called 'bolt-and-shutter maintaining power' device – that successfully solved the problem of maintaining the power supply (or driving force) when rewinding the clock. Indeed, the clock cannot be wound without activating an ancillary spring that gives enough additional power to keep the clock going while the rewinding is taking place.

This clock (*inside back cover*) shows the trend for highly decorative cases that quickly became fashionable. Both in England and on the Continent, particularly in Holland, marquetry was admired and the long-case of this clock (6ft 10in high) has an olivewood veneer inlaid with star medallions of ebony and satinwood. These beautiful English domestic long-case striking clocks, however, rarely have marquetry that can rival in quality and virtuosity the long-case of the Dutch clock by Jacob Hasius (*fig. 62*), which stands 7ft 2in high. This Amsterdam maker (active 1682–1725) has provided a movement comparable to Tompion's work, but it has only an eight-day duration.

The domestic clock reached extraordinary heights of complexity and beauty in England under the patronage of the court and the aristocracy in the decades around 1700. The magnificent year-going clock by Daniel Quare

(*fig. 62*) is housed in a tall walnut case (9ft 10in high) with gilt-brass mounts of intricate and beautiful design. The dial has elaborate cast spandrels incorporating the Royal Arms at the top and it is said that this clock may have been made for Hampton Court Palace. Certainly it contains a rare refinement – an additional movement, with its dial situated in the door of the trunk of the case, to provide the so-called equation of time, that is, the relationship between mean time and solar time. Few clocks with equation movements have survived and Daniel Quare, who became a Free Brother of the Company in 1671, was one of the more significant contributors to the rise of London's supremacy in the horological field at this time. He died in 1724 and was buried in the Quaker's Burial Ground at Bunhill Fields; all his life he was a stout protagonist of his religious beliefs.

At about this time, during the last quarter of the seventeenth century, a considerable demand for night clocks must have arisen, for in the 1650s the first clocks designed to be read in the dark and at a distance were made. They seem to have been an Italian invention, perhaps the creation of Johann Philip Treffler, who worked for the Archduke Ferdinand II of Tuscany. The Museum's magnificent example (*fig. 63*) is signed on the back of the movement: *'Petrus Thomas Campanus, Inventor, Roma, 1683'*. Pietro Campani's invention was indeed clever because he solved the problem of the noise of the clock disturbing the sleeper at night. His pendulum controlled movement actuated an eccentric balance which has a continuous – not an intermittent – motion and so resulted in an

**62** Three long-case clocks, *c.* 1700–1730: (*from left to right*) a Dutch marquetry eight-day clock by Jacob Hasius, of Amsterdam; an English walnut-veneered year-going Equation Clock by Daniel Quare, height 9 ft 10 in (300 cm); an English mahogany and silver month-going Equation Regulator by George Graham. *All formerly in the Ilbert Collection; given by Mr Gilbert Edgar, C.B.E. in 1958.*

almost entirely silent movement. The latter is small but the clock case itself was made to house more than just the movement: like all these early night-clocks – and there are many contemporary English versions, including one long-case example by Edward East (in the British Museum) – Pietro Campani's version accommodated a lamp, a reflector and a chimney, so that a bright light would shine through the pierced numerals of the rotating hours as one by one they came in line with the beam of light. Although the problem of noisy movements may have been solved by Pietro Campani, the great danger of fire from a light left burning all night was, however, very real and once again the circle of leading London clockmakers found a solution – 'repeating-work'. By pulling a little cord at the side of the clock, the repeat mechanism would be released and the clock would strike the last hour and the last quarter, so the listener would know the time – at least it would be correct within a quarter of an hour. This solution was incorporated into Tompion's greatest masterpiece – his Royal year-going

**66** Detail of the Royal Tompion Clock (*see fig. 64*), showing the Royal coat-of-arms as borne for a few months in the middle of the year 1689.

spring-driven clock that until 1982 had belonged to Lord Mostyn (*figs. 64, 65a, 65b, 66*).

In this clock, Tompion succeeded in producing the earliest known spring-driven pendulum clock designed to go for a year and also to strike the hours for a year on one winding and, when the pull repeating mechanism is operated, to strike the quarters which automatically leads to the release of the hour-striking mechanism, so that the last hour is also repeated. This achievement remained unique, certainly until the nineteenth century.

Tompion's *tour de force* is signed twice; once on the dial and again on the front-plate, which has matchless engraved ornament in the full-blooded Baroque manner of the finest Continental designs. The entire case of veneered ebony and silver mounts is of regal excellence and, significantly, it is surmounted by a silver figure of Britannia, flanked by four silver finials – the rose (of England) and the thistle (of Scotland), the lion and the unicorn (the royal supporters). In the centre is the silver crowned shield bearing the Royal Arms (*fig. 66*).

Hitherto, these Arms have always been published as those of King William III and, therefore, been dated after the death of his wife, Queen Mary, who died in Kensington Palace in December 1694. In fact, the coat of arms is a very rare form of the Royal Arms which was only in use for a few months in the first year of their reign, namely, from 11 April 1689 (when the Scottish parliament eventually agreed to recognise the joint monarchy of William and Mary) until the autumn of 1689 (when a very different and final version comprising the Stuart Arms with those of Nassau was adopted). As this final version continued unchanged until William III's death in 1702, this clock must have been designed in mid 1689. Indeed, the theme of the decorations of his Tompion clock seems to celebrate this Scottish acceptance which, by coincidence, occurred on the day of their coronation in Westminster, 11 April 1689.

In the same year William III purchased the house that was to become Kensington Palace and by October 1689 the work of conversion was under way, with the Queen personally

**64** *left*. Tompion's Royal Clock of 1689, the year of the Coronation of Mary (daughter of James II) and William III (of Orange). The silver figure of Britannia, holding a shield bearing the combined crosses of St George and St Andrew, is flanked at the four corners by the silver rose (for England), the silver thistle (for Scotland) and the silver lion and unicorn (the Royal Supporters).

The clock was made for the Royal Bedchamber in Kensington Palace. It is the first pendulum-controlled spring-driven clock to go for one year without rewinding and has a pull repeating mechanism that sounds the last quarter and the last hour struck – a most desirable refinement during the hours of darkness. On the King's death in 1702, it passed to the Earl of Romney, Gentleman of the Bedchamber and so by descent to the present Lord Mostyn. Height 28 in (71 cm). *Purchased in 1982.*

**65a** *right*. Detail of the Royal Tompion Clock (fig. 64) showing the dial (5 x 5 in; 12.7 x 12.7 cm) with its silver spandrels, the blued-steel hour and counterpoised minute hands, and the aperture through which is revealed the revolving silver disc engraved with the days of the week and their appropriate planets in emblematic forms.

**65b** *right below*. Front-plate of the movement of the Royal Tompion Clock (see *inside front cover*) engraved with the signature in the central cartouche; the unrecorded artist was one of the finest craftsmen of his day and this front-plate has been compared with the remarkable engraving on the silver table at Chatsworth which is signed *'B. Gentot In. Fecit'*, but the evidence is inconclusive.

supervising all the alterations and furnishings. In the list of items in the Queen's bedchamber (made shortly after her death) there is a note: 'one fine clock upon a carved pedestall (this clock in ye King's bedchamber)'. Evidently, the King had it transferred immediately the Queen died and in the 1697 Inventory of the King's new bedchamber is listed: 'one fine silver clock out of ye Queen's old bedchamber'.

When William III died in 1702, the contents of the Royal Bedchamber went, as a perquisite to Henry Sydney, Earl of Romney, Gentleman of the Bedchamber and Groom of the Stole. On his death two years later, the clock passed to the Fifth Earl of Leicester and so by descent to Lord

Mostyn's family, who since 1793 have kept a written record of the clock's performance and annual rewinding.

The massive driving work of Tompion's movement with its twin barrels, and reversed fusees (*inside front cover*) terminates in a truly delicate verge escapement. The dial is mounted on the upper part, which is a subsidiary assembly that carries the remainder of all three trains, together with the repeat bar on the front-plate and the hour bell on the back-plate.

Verge escapements continued to be used in domestic clocks, especially the so-called bracket-clocks, because they were intended to be portable – at least, easy to move from one room to another or one house to another. The precision pendulum escapements and even the anchor escapement had to be placed on an absolutely level surface to obtain good results. Their sensitiveness to the positioning made them unsuitable for the rigours of domestic use.

For scientific work, especially in observatories, greater accuracy was required than could be provided by the anchor (or recoil) escapement. Tompion, in his 1675–6 Greenwich 'Great Clocks', seems to have invented a pinwheel form of escapement that may have been, in some sense, a precursor of the 'dead-beat' escapement – known more correctly as 'Graham's dead-beat escapement' (*fig. 68*). In 1715 George Graham invented an escapement which gives to the pendulum an impulse when it nears the zero position and only produces a frictional drag elsewhere. The pallets are so designed that there is no longer a recoil, and the seconds-hand, therefore, does not bounce back, as on any ordinary long-case clock – hence the term 'dead-beat'.

George Graham's long-case equation clock (*fig. 62*) made about 1730, incorporated his new invention. This clock, 7ft 8in high, is a one month regulator, with an annual calendar, a concentric gilt minute-hand showing solar time, a concentric steel minute-hand showing mean time, and above, on the semi-circular dial, equation and calendar date. Within the long-case are hung the weight and the temperature-compensated pendulum. Mercury pendulums

**67** One of the two 'Great Clocks' made by Thomas Tompion for the Royal Observatory, Greenwich, in 1675–6. Designed to go for a year without rewinding, and with a 13ft-long pendulum suspended *above* the movement and beating every two seconds. Height 12½ in (32 cm). *Purchased in 1928.*

**69** *far right.* 'The Great Room' in the Royal Observatory in Greenwich, built in 1675 by Sir Christopher Wren for the first Astronomer Royal, John Flamsteed. An etching by Francis Place, *c.* 1676, shows the two 'Great Clocks' to the left of the door, with the pendulum bobs above the dials. The dial on the Museum's clock is engraved: 'Sir Jonas Moore Caused this Movement with great Care to be thus Made. A° 1676 by Tho. Tompion'.

**68** *right.* Diagram of Graham's 'dead-beat' escapement.

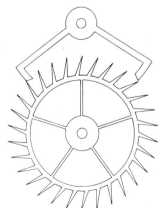

had been invented in 1726 by George Graham and combined with 'dead-beat' escapements produced a degree of accuracy in timekeeping which was of the greatest benefit in observatories but was also used in many domestic clocks.

George Graham died in 1751, when he was nearly eighty, and was buried in Tompion's grave in Westminster Abbey. He had joined Tompion soon after he was free of the Company in 1695 and married Tompion's niece in 1704. Having entered into partnership with Tompion, he inherited the flourishing concern, became Master of the Company in 1720, and as a Fellow of the Royal Society contributed many learned papers. He perfected a new form of escapement for watchwork and after 1725 his watches tend to be designed with the 'cylinder' escapement, in which the escape-wheel works in a horizontal plane – hence sometimes referred to as the 'horizontal' escapement. In fact, the cylinder escapement became *de rigueur* in expensive eighteenth-century watches but it was extremely difficult to make. To minimise wear, the acting surfaces were later made of a precious hardstone – hence the famous variant known as the ruby cylinder.

The most handsome example of the use of the cylinder escapement occurs in a watch that has survived with its chatelaine (*see title page*). The movement with quarter-repeating work is signed 'J. Leroux No. 2979 London', while the dust-cap is engraved 'Jn. Leroux Charing Cross London'. The gold case has London hallmarks for 1778 and the enamelling on the outer gold case and the chatelaine are signed by William Craft and dated 1777. Craft was a regular exhibitor at the Royal Academy between 1774 and 1781 and again in the nineties, but on this chatelaine and watch-case he has painted *en grisaille* in the Neo-classical style, producing a cameo-like effect which is particularly effective in the portraits of King George III and Queen Charlotte. The watch and chatelaine were made for Sir James Napier, F.R.S., F.S.A., who in March 1778 was in London to receive his knighthood, after a long career as Inspector-General of His Majesty's Hospitals in North America. Sir James, who had opened an account with Coutts Bank in the Strand in 1754, made one payment to John Leroux; it was for the sum of sixty-three pounds and ten shillings on 27 February 1779. As John Arnold, the celebrated chronometer maker, charged 150 guineas for his best gold repeaters in 1791, this payment by Sir James must refer to this watch.

Although John Leroux, a maker of French origin, was already established in London by 1744, he was not admitted into Clockmakers' Company until 1781. Nevertheless his surviving work is without exception of very high quality, and the Museum was fortunate to purchase this historic watch and chatelaine in 1979. He was, in fact, a maker of outstanding ability and almost unique among London makers of the eighteenth century in appreciating and improving upon the lever escapement invented by Thomas Mudge in 1754 – perhaps the most successful of all watch escapements.

Thomas Mudge (1715–94) completed his apprenticeship with George Graham in 1738 and thereafter frequently used Graham's cylinder escapement. But in his pursuit of finding the longitude with the aid of a timepiece, Mudge had already produced a drawing of a new escapement, which was seen and no doubt much discussed by Johann Huber, the Swiss astronomer, during his four-month visit to Mudge in 1754. The results were to be incorporated into Mudge's celebrated 'lever' table-clock with its skilful use of a remontoire and large, heavy balance, its temperature compensation for the balance and its safeguards against friction (*figs. 70, 71*). Although this clock with its lunar train and dial had a new form of escapement capable of remarkably precise timekeeping, there is no evidence to confirm that Mudge intended it to compete for the Board of Longitude's Prize of £20,000, nor that its performance was ever recorded by Mudge or his contemporaries.

When he was nearly sixty, Mudge finished his marine timekeeper 'No. 1' (*fig. 70*) and three years later, in 1777, his other two marine chronometers, known as 'Green' and 'Blue' (after the colour of their cases). Their performance during the tests was better than any of the rivals submitted by his English contemporaries, but without his supervision they tended to develop troubles and in the end Mudge only received £2,500 as a result of a decision in Parliament. His three marine timepieces are marvels of complex clockmaking and, significantly, his son's scheme to market a range of copies, with the aid of the best craftsmen and his aged father's advice, failed because none was capable of as good a performance as the originals, in which Mudge's 'constant force escapement' had made history.

Mudge's great rival was John Arnold (1736–99), who had as a young man made a considerable stir when in 1764 he presented George III with a ruby cylinder watch complete with repeating mechanism set in a case less than an inch across. This feat was followed by his perfection of the chronometer, (or spring-detent) escapement, by which he so freed the balance for the greater part of its swing that he was to make a watch that never exceeded an error of three seconds per day throughout its year of testing. By 1784 he had invented the gold helical spring and made several impressive improvements to the design of the balance, using two different metals. In the fifty-hour 'Expedition' marine chronometer 'No. 14/104' (*fig. 70*), Arnold introduced for the first time a combination of silver and platinum. This chronometer was being made by Arnold in 1790 (the date and the name of his assistant, John Glover, are on the great wheel) when, on the order of the Board of Longitude, it had to be completed in time to join Captain Vancouver's ship. It was to be away from England for four years until September 1795, having circumnavigated the globe once, sailed twice to Hawaii and as far north along the western coast of North America as Cook Inlet in Alaska, in the most gruelling conditions. Throughout this period it was in constant use during astronomical observations made on shore, and its performance was systematically recorded by Captain Vancouver.

The Canadian city that bears his name as well as the Island of Vancouver were charted during this pioneering Expedition, and recently the companion Arnold chonometer ('No. 176') which spent the same four years on Captain Vancouver's ship returned to the City of Vancouver to join the collections at the Maritime Museum.

John Arnold, whose reputation on the Continent was very great, attracted the esteem and close friendship of the slightly younger Abraham-Louis Breguet (1747–1823). This genius, many would claim the greatest in this field of horology ever to have lived, came from Neuchâtel in Switzerland and was married and installed in his own premises in Paris by 1775. Within five years his reputation was firmly established. Perhaps one of the most evocative creations is the little silver-cased watch (*fig. 70*) which Breguet gave in 1809 to Arnold's son, John Roger, as a tribute to the revered memory of his father. This watch has an inscribed silver plate (attached to the top-plate of the movement) that records that it is one of the first of John Arnold's watches, and was later fitted with the first *tourbillon* regulator ever made by Breguet. Its design enabled the entire balance and the escapement to revolve, thereby eliminating those positional errors that occur when a watch movement is not horizontal. The Paris goldsmith Etienne Tavernier made the engine-turned case for Breguet at the end of 1808.

Not only did Breguet contribute on a technical level with a series of new improvements and inventions, but he transformed their appearance, so that superb timekeeping qualities were married to an elegant simplicity of design. Whilst this is particularly true of his watches, it is to be seen even in the very few extant observatory clocks. An example (*fig. 72*), signed 'Breguet et Fils' and dating from about 1815, was designed to strike each second – a true precursor of today's time-signal. The 'constant force' escapement can be seen through the opening in the dial and the temperature-compensated 'Harrison' grid-iron pendulum is surmounted by a regulator carrying two tiny balls, which can be seen under its little glass dome. The performance of this clock would have greatly facilitated any scientific study of the transit of the stars, and its austere wood case and crisp marking of the dials combine to

**70** Four precision timepieces of the second half of the eighteenth century: (*from left to right*) the unique 'lever' table-clock by Thomas Mudge in its arched glazed case, height 12 in (30.5 cm); the celebrated 'First Marine Timekeeper' of Thomas Mudge with the movement (shown out of its glazed octagonal mahogany case) – a brilliant contestant for the Board of Longitude's Award of £10,000 in 1774; the marine chronometer No. 14/104 by John Arnold, who made it for Captain Vancouver's famous expedition to the north-west coast of North America in 1791–5 and incorporated for the first time both silver and platinum in his design for the balance; a small watch by Arnold senior in an engine-turned silver case which Abraham-Louis Breguet gave to John Roger Arnold in 1809, having fitted it with his first *tourbillon* regulator. The inscription begins: '*Hommage de Breguet a la memoire reverée d'Arnold . . .*' *All from the Ilbert Collection; given by Mr Gilbert Edgar, C.B.E. in 1958.*

**71** The movement of the Thomas Mudge 'lever' table-clock (*see fig. 70*), with its large heavy balance and remontoire, which is rewound every 7½ minutes; the lunar mechanism has as little error as 0.2 of a second per lunation – the most successful achievement in a portable clock.

give it a quality of harmony as well.

The same characteristically good design can be noted in the watches of Breguet in the Museum's collection, and Breguet's influence had a long-lasting effect on French and Swiss watchmaking. In the mid-nineteenth-century Swiss watch (*title page*) signed 'Bovet Fleurier' (a family firm in Fleurier, near Neuchâtel), the layout of the fine movement has bars and cocks in place of the solid top-plate recalling the 'Lepine/Breguet' style of the late eighteenth century. This design enabled the watch to be more slim and, because the Bovet firm was the chief supplier of watches to China at this time, the entire surface of the movement has been ornately silvered, gilded, enamelled and engraved. The outer case with its border of pearls is typical of the technically brilliant enamelling of the Swiss workshops, though its lack of good design is symptomatic of the decline that followed in the wake of the expansion of the watch industry in Switzerland.

In London, the firm of Sir John Bennett (active from 1843) was among the first to import Swiss watch mechanisms in quantity and then add the finishing touches in his own London workshops, put them in handsome cases and sell them as the products of the firm. Bennett recognised the power of advertising, and in 1851 at the Great Exhibition spent lavishly to boost his firm's name, for he more than any other English maker recognised the danger of the growing competition from Switzerland. In 1872 he received his knighthood, and he was awarded the Silver Medal at the Paris Exhibition of 1878, for which this armorial watch was apparently made (*title page*). The movement is

**72** An observatory clock signed *'Breguet et Fils'*; it is designed to strike each second. The 'constant force' escapement, the temperature-compensated Harrison grid-iron pendulum and the regulator with its two tiny balls under the glass dome combine to make this instrument immensely reliable for recording anywhere on the earth's surface the movements of the stars. Height 16¾ in (42.5 cm). *From the Ilbert Collection; given by Mr Gilbert Edgar, C.B.E. in 1958.*

a most rare example of the most developed and sophisticated striking work ever incorporated into a watch. In the design and layout of the lever escapement it is more in the Swiss than the English tradition and was either the work of a Swiss craftsman in Bennett's employ or, more probably, imported.

The watch not only strikes the hours and the quarters but its repeating mechanism enables the wearer to hear the last hour, the last quarter and the last minute repeated on the wire-gongs with their differing pitch. The latter were first introduced by Breguet. The richly enamelled case has various armorial devices relating to the City of London, but principally it bears the arms of Sir John Bennett, with his motto and monogram – all in the Neo-Gothic style.

Under Breguet's influence the French taste for 'skeleton' clocks of the late eighteenth century became extremely popular throughout Europe, but expecially in London in the nineteenth century. One particularly fascinating example is the so-called 'rolling ball' clock which S.J.M. French of The Royal Exchange made about 1810 (fig. 73). In its veneered case with glass dome this clock has become an object of light-hearted enjoyment, but it was based on a very serious attempt by Sir William Congreve to produce a perfect timekeeper. In 1808 Congreve patented his invention, 'a clock with a ball rolling down an inclined plane', and his model, driven by weights, is still preserved in the Rotunda at Woolwich.

More than a century and a half after George Graham's brilliant achievements of the 1720s, the last significant improvement in the degree of accuracy in the time-keeping of 'mechanical' precision clocks was achieved by Riefler. (A modern example of Riefler's escapement can be seen in the Gallery of Clocks and Watches.) Riefler's clocks were introduced into observatories around the world, until superseded by Shortt's electrical 'free pendulum clock' in the mid-1920s. Only in 1942 was their place taken by the quartz-crystal controlled clocks. These modern developments fall outside the scope of this book, which has been concerned with the harnessing of the power of the falling weight and the unwinding spring in the task of measuring and recording time.

In the domestic market, however, the 'mechanical' time-piece has never lost favour, although both electric (mains and battery) and quartz-crystal timepieces have become rivals. The latter tend to be regarded as 'expendable' and so for presentation purposes or for lasting quality, the mechanical clock, especially the so-called 'carriage-clocks' in the tradition of Breguet, have continued to be made by craftsmen in many countries, often incorporating technical improvements designed to make the mechanism run for longer periods.

Similarly, the history of the mechanical watch continues up to the fifties when the first electrically powered watches appeared, only to be overtaken by the quartz-crystal controlled watch ten years later. Perhaps the most far-reaching development came during the First World War when the wrist-watch first became accepted. Subsequently, its popularity led to many improvements – self-winding, waterproof and, even, shockproof watches have been produced.

The watch, once an object of luxury, became available to all because of techniques evolved in the late nineteenth century that made mass-production possible. This revolution of the watchmaking trade began in the USA but was quickly developed by the Swiss and in the year 1898, for example, Ingersoll sold one million pocket watches, mostly made for them by Waterbury & Co.

The merits of a 'mechanical' timepiece – be it a clock or a watch – continue to be appreciated and today craftsmen of the highest calibre are still improving on the attainments of the 'old masters', aiming to reduce, for example, the need for lubrication and, hence, for regular maintenance. The story of mechanical time-keeping is not closed.

**73** 'Clock with ball rolling down an incline plane', as William Congreve described it in his patent of 1808; this example is signed *'French, Royal Exchange. No. 470'* and dates from about 1810, together with its satinwood glazed case. The base is 17 x 17 in square (43.2 x 43.2 cm). *From the Ilbert Collection; given by Mr Gilbert Edgar, C.B.E. in 1958.*

# Further Reading

Some general and specialist books in English, published (or reprinted) since 1970 – and hence more readily available – have been selected. The list has been arranged to follow the order of the text of this book; detailed bibliographies may be found in the publications mentioned below.

J.D. NORTH, *Richard of Wallingford*, 3 vols (Oxford, 1976)

W.G.C. BACKINSELL, *The Medieval Clock in Salisbury Cathedral*, (South Wiltshire Industrial Archaeology Society, 1978)

C.F.C. BEESON, *English Church Clocks, 1280–1850*, (London, revised 1977)

G.H. BAILLIE, A.H. LLOYD, F.A.B. WARD, *The Planetarium of Giovannie di Dondi, Citizen of Padua*, (London, 1974)

H.C. KING and J.R. MILLBURN, *Geared to the Stars* (Bristol, USA., 1978)

J.H. LEOPOLD, *The Almanus Manuscript*, (London, 1971)

(Edited by) KLAUS MAURICE and OTTO MAYR, *The Clockwork Universe – German Clocks and Automata 1550–1650*, (New York, 1980)

P.G. COOLE and E. NEUMANN, *The Orpheus Clocks*, (London 1972)

G.H. BAILLIE, *Watches* (A facsimile reprint by the N.A.G. Press of the original 1929 edition; London, 1979)

C. CLUTTON and G. DANIELS, *Watches*, (London, 1979)

P.M. CHAMBERLAIN, *It's About Time* (A facsimile reprint by Holland Press of the original 1941 edition; London, 1978)

J.L. SELLINK, *Dutch Antique Domestic Clocks*, (Leiden, 1975)

R. PLOMP, *Spring-driven Dutch Pendulum Clocks, 1657–1710* (Schiedam, 1979)

T. ROBINSON, *The Longcase Clock*, (Woodbridge, 1981)

P. DAWSON, C. DROVER, D. PARKES, *Early English Clocks*, (Woodbridge, 1982)

EDOUARD PHILLIPS, *Treatise on the Balance-Spring* (Trans. by Dr J.D. Weaver; Monograph No. 15, Antiquarian Horological Society, n.d.)

D. HOWSE, *Greenwich Time and the discovery of the longitude* (Oxford, 1980)

*Pioneers of Precision Timekeeping*, (Monograph No. 3, The Antiquarian Horological Society, (n.d.)

THOMAS MUDGE, Junior, *A Description . . . . (Mudge on Timekeepers)*; a facsimile reprint of the 1799 edition (London, 1977)

R.T. GOULD, *The Marine Chronometer; its history and development*, (London, reprinted 1971)

V. MERCER, *John Arnold and Son, Chronometer Makers, 1762–1843*, (London, 1972)

G. DANIELS, *The Art of Breguet*, (London, 1975)

E. JAQUET and A. CHAPUIS, *The Technique and History of the Swiss Watch*, (London, 1970)

F.A.B. WARD, *Time Measurement, an Historical Review*, (Science Museum, London, 1970)

A. SMITH (Edited by), *Dictionary of Clocks*, (London, 1979)

F.A.B. WARD, *Clocks and Watches: I Weight-driven Clocks*, (Science Museum, London, 1973); *II Spring-driven Clocks*, (Science Museum, London, 1972)

F. MADDISON and A.J. TURNER, *A Catalogue of watches in the Museum of the History of Science, Oxford*, (Oxford, 1973)

C. CLUTTON and G. DANIEL, *The Collection of the Clockmakers' Company*, (London, 1975)

## Reference Works on Makers, and Mechanical and Technical Aspects:

(a) G.H. BAILLIE: *Watchmakers and Clockmakers of the World* (reprinted by the N.A.G. Press Ltd., London). For Vol. 2 see next entry.

(b) B. LOOMES, *Watchmakers and Clockmakers of the World*, Vol. 2, (London, 1976)

(c) B. LOOMES, *The Early Clockmakers of Great Britain*, (London, 1981)

(d) C. CLUTTON, G.H. BAILLIE and C.A. ILBERT, *Britten's Old Clocks and Watches and their Makers*, 8th Edition, (London, 1973)

(e) W.J. GAZELEY, *Clock and Watch Escapements*, (London, re-printed 1980)

(f) G. DANIELS, *Watchmaking*, (London, 1982)

(g) G.H. BAILLIE, *Clocks and Watches: An Historical Bibliography* (London, re-printed 1978)

# Index